BEAUTIFUL

The Awakening

By A.T. Waters

Beautiful: The Awakening

Portland, Oregon

ISBN 979-8-9853029-0-5

Cover Photo by Harrison Haines

Contents

Forward

When God wakes you in the night and says, "Write." I have learned that the best thing to do is open your eyes and obey. Don't look at the clock and roll your eyes when you see it is 2:45, and then roll over and go back to sleep. He will wake you again until you write. This book has been just that, a long series of thoughts written down as I have been roused at around the 2:45 mark night after night in half an hour to two hour increments. I wouldn't trade all the sleep in the world for the words that you are about to read. They are the heart of me, but I believe they are also the very heart of God.

I have never had words come so fast, so in order, so concise and revealing. I actually was writing another book when all this began to pour forth on its own. It too covers my life journey and themes of living, dying, love, and vulnerability, but there was just something about the journey that God desired to make known. And maybe that is why He woke me... so that the words were His and not mine.

I like to think, to ponder, to solve all of life's little mysteries. God knew that I was a fine writer and my thoughts would be accurate and adequate, but He also knew my mind would second guess, over think, and analyze every word. Writing whatever comes to the forefront of your mind is an exercise in surrender, and every morning when I woke up and read what had been written in the wee hours of the night, I was in awe...

So, as you read the following it may seem a bit stream of consciousness at times and the imagery may overtake the story. It may force you to go back and reread paragraphs or sections. I make no apologies. I wanted to keep the text as true to the spirit of how it was conceived as possible. There are realities that may or may not be true to you as you read--words that will bring a sense of discomfort. I hope in those moments you will listen to the stirring in your soul and investigate “the why”. It was those very questions that set me out on my journey. May it open a door to you as well...

CHAPTER 1

Am I Dead Yet?

"The cords and sorrows of death encompassed me, And the terrors of Sheol came upon me; I found distress and sorrow."

~PSALM 116:3 AMP

There are stories and then there are stories, and when a story is a good story it is a much shared story and a story that haunts you and you can't put it down. I feel like this is how my life has been for the last few months--a story that neither I nor those around me dare put down. There is a looming suspense; a question of authentic change, a wondering if this is, in fact, real. As the main character in this sorted tale, I can tell you it is more real than anything I have ever known, yet so otherworldly that I too question the authenticity.

Had you told me even six months ago that life would reflect the image I see before me today I would have laughed, somewhat hysterically, at you. It is not that I didn't believe that God could change my heart, heal my brokenness, or remold my thinking. It was just that my imagination was too finite to create an image to compare to the life I am living today or to even conjure up the journey to get here. I wake up every morning and wonder...*Who am I today? What crazy thing is going to happen next? Is it Monday or Tuesday?*

It is hard to explain life to someone when days are more like years and months are like lifetimes. I truly feel like I have lived a few lifetimes in the past months. My friends say it is a miracle, like watching a butterfly come to life. They use words like brave and courageous and miracle, but it doesn't seem like any of those things. It just feels like living.

Most stories are about living. It is interesting to think that we don't read stories about something that is dead, unless we are reading about the character leading up to said death, or the lives affected thereafter. Nobody cares to get into the mind of a dead thing and wander around in the emptiness of their thoughts. It is dull, lifeless really. It is nothing more than a void and a void, a big empty void, was where I feel like I crawled out of...

They say no one knows death until they die. I have to disagree with the statement because I feel very much like I know what death feels like and I am still very much alive, but I will say I did not know what life was until I rose from the grip of death. To not feel, to not know love, that was death. I knew death well. We were good friends.

Making friends with death was not on my “to do” list when I set out on this journey of life. Death chose me over and over, courting me until I broke off the relationship only to embrace me once again in his waiting arms. It was a tragic relationship actually, much like one of those movies where the lead character dies of some unnamed cancer, except in my story there were no tears, there was no feeling. Whether I chose death or death chose me matters little when in the end you lose everything. What I did not realize was what I had to lose.

Identity, when you don’t have one to call your own, becomes a life quest to find one. You put on an outfit, look at yourself in the mirror, and depending on whether you like what you see or not you decide your next step--your next layer of life. And that was what my identity was built on, not a revealing of the heart of me, but a dance and a game to tame the voices that hurled their painful words. The funny thing about not having an identity all your own, you will go to the ends of the earth to find it, transposing notes of authenticity into a key you can’t quite vocalize, but seems much easier for others to sing. It sounds harmonious at first, but then the notes soon ring dissonant.

I have always hated singing the “Happy Birthday” song. It always felt inauthentic and ritualistic, as did birthdays in general. My long awaited third birthday delivered a lifetime gift. A brother.

There is something about having a brother born on your birthday that just robs you unknowingly. At the moment it is more wonderful than you could ever imagine, but as time goes on you realize that that single moment in time stripped something from you. “I” would always be “we”, and identity, true individuality, ceased to exist. Finding “me” would be an epic journey complete with an archaeological excavation to uncover the heart buried decades before.

Digging in the dirt is not for the faint of heart, there are bugs, worms, creepy things. But if you dig long enough and in the right place you may find a treasure. My brother and I spent a lot of time back by the old wood pile, me sifting dirt and him playing with his oversized excavation toys. With my screen across my yellow bucket I would shake and sift the dirt until the rocks sat on the screen and the fluffy brown soil filled my bucket. It almost went without saying as I carefully poured the water in, the next step was to slather the perfectly smooth mud all over our exposed limbs and wait for it to dry. Then, after sitting still until our shell was complete, we would flex and watch the hardened mud crumble off just like the Incredible Hulk coming to life. I will not lie, I was not a princess and we were not inventing facial mud, we were imagining our alter egos waking. Plain and simple.

Most little girls play dress up and long to be princesses in flowing gowns with a prince on their arm. I had no clue such things went on. It was all cowboys and Indians, matchbox cars and Legos in my world. I wasn't exactly a tomboy, but I wasn't a girly girl either. I was rough and tumble with a soft sensitive core that I wouldn't let you see, but at times I could feel it so deeply it nearly wrecked me. And in times of stress, like the Hulk, it was the anger that came to the surface. I tried to keep it down, but the mud would crack and my angst would be seen, I would be ashamed for my outbursts, and retreat into my quiet places. I wasn't dead yet, just dying.

The process of death is gradual. Once the disease takes hold it can be many years before the symptoms warrant your attention and the diagnosis made. Looking back through the looking glass and seeing life for all it was, I can see the disease permeating my tissue, drawing life from my viable frame. But at the time I appeared to be just a vivacious little girl, a bit bossy, overly talkative, energetic, curious, and unusually secretive.

Little Miss Bossy came on the scene with a vengeance, demanding the submission of all the serfs in her kingdom. At three I found my first subject in my little kingdom, and though I loved him greatly, I sought to control my brother's every move. I was his protector, his comforter, his provider, the ruler of the province. The delusion of grandeur laid upon me as I sought my royal post, but as I grasped for more and more control my tiny hands grew strong and my heart grew hard. I wanted to be in control, but I had no aspirations to be a princess...more like Joan of Arc or Amelia Earhart--independent, strong, resilient. (If you remember, things didn't turn out too well for either of them.)

Growing up my brother and I were close and the best of friends. When I would come home from college we would sit and talk for hours. My mother always wondered aloud what it was we could be talking about for so long. There was a kinship, through the good and bad seasons, that instilled in us a trust and love that nothing was able to rival. Private things remained deep within, but there was a knowing. A knowing that we weren't alone. It was much like I imagine twins feeling, like the other part of you is really in someone else.

It is a fantasy of sorts to grow up thinking that you have a twin somewhere, and like in the Parent Trap you will just happen to run into them someday. I was pretty sure that the hole I felt within was just that, my long lost other half. The chasm was deep and empty, and beckoned to be filled, but seemed bottomless. It felt like weakness.

Weakness and its competitor strength warred within me in unending battles for my attention. I would feel weak and pull myself up by my bootstraps to prove my strength. I would glow with pride in my strength and feel inadequate and weak under it all. I would find myself shattered and refuse to let the tears come.

Tears were the ultimate sign of weakness, so I disallowed tears. I would feel the emotions rising up within me and push them down, further and further, hoping that my efforts would keep even the littlest of tears from finding my eyelids. I only remember crying a handful of times in my life, and most of them recently. Tears drew attention and required the acceptance of my lack and need. It made already uncomfortable feelings even more troublesome. I never wanted to be seen as needy, and actually, I didn't really want to be seen even though I did everything in my power to be the center of attention. Even from my earliest years I was satisfied to take care of myself. For all intents and purposes I was self-made (or at least I thought).

Being self-made comes with the folly of a child-like mind deciding what is best for the long term success of growth and development. I don't care how smart you are at five years old, you will have no idea how to choose the right path to get you where you need to go. That is why God created parents, grandparents, teachers, coaches... A child is not meant to be an adult or God would have had us come out of the womb eighteen years old and equipped to take on the world. We're not. So to take hold of one's life at such a young age is a setup for ultimate failure.

I was a pretty independent, but obedient child. I did as I was told, but I was never the child to ask for help. To place a memory on my childhood would look something like a little strawberry blonde girl dangling from the limbs of a tree, or riding a two-wheeler with a teddy bear bungeed to the back of her seat. There was a carefree wildness to her that cried out for adventure as she endlessly chattered and stuttered through her thoughts. She had an awe about everything and a question about everything else.

It would be the questions that would haunt her as the years passed. *Why did her mind leave her in times of stress? Where did the anxiety come from? Why did thunder and lightning shake her to the core even years after childhood was a distant memory? Why did every touch seem sexual and wrong? Where was everybody? Why am I always alone?*

It was the last question that sunk like a stone to the pit of my stomach. The other questions I was comfortable not knowing the answer to, but the question of alone, that one stuck with me. It stuck to me like duct tape across my mouth keeping me from asking any further questions. But even without the words coming from my mouth, my mind whirled in ebbing tides of confusion as I tried to determine what it was that made me so alone; what strange force was at work always banishing me to this secluded island, and if ever there would be a moment of rescue. I gave up on rescue early on and resorted to self-sufficiency as I built my raft and planned my escape.

The mind of a child is in fact childish. There is plenty of fantasy and fiction and very little in the way of practical or well engineered thinking. I spent a lot of time in the trees; some would say my head in the clouds. It was not uncommon for me to spend hours reading, writing, or just dreaming about who knows what as I perched in the branches of that silly dogwood. You would have thought I was at the top of the mighty oak the way I escaped to my spot. But the oak was too tall and had no limbs low enough for me to reach, the dogwood was much more manageable. It became my refuge.

There was a safety among the branches and leaves that few other places seemed to hold. No one could come up unless I said they could and no one really wanted to come up, except my brother and maybe my friend. That was, until they realized that there was really only room for one in the tree. And that was yet another beginning of death.

Now death as a noun is something like dying, but it is not active like dying. It is not a process. It is definitive. It declares the end of something. And somewhere around the discovery of alone I contracted a disease; a cancer really, that sought to steal my life one bit at a time until I was all used up.

For some people they look back through life and see smiles, birthday cakes, snuggles on the couch, and warm hugs and kisses and goodbyes. I think about Christmases and I remember swimming through toys and boxes and wrapping paper. Stuff. Birthdays were not that special either, lots of cake. I am really not a big fan of cake. And movie nights, well they were times to throw a sleeping bag on the floor and fall asleep to the flicker of the old T.V. when the VHS came to its end. I really don't remember people. I guess they were probably there. I know my brother was there. I loved my brother very much. He was my world when I was not my world. But the feeling I have when I reflect on those early years is lonely.

Had you asked me years ago if I was, or had ever felt, lonely, I would have categorically denied such a thing. The truth is, being dead has a way of shaping your world view and though I did not know it, my aloneness was what accentuated my morbid reality. The whole world knew it. They all knew and no one even thought to do CPR. Of course, it is hard to save the life of someone who didn't need saving, or at least looked like they were not in distress. They knew something wasn't right, but then again nothing seemed wrong either. I was a zombie walking through life with a really clean set of clothes and a nice smile. Just don't touch me because my arm might come loose in your hand.

I would say it is safe to classify most of my life as sleepwalking. When I was a kid I did a lot of sleepwalking, sleep talking, and wetting the bed. I hated wetting the bed. It was like the epitome of failure and yet I had no clue how to avoid it. I remember one summer camping in my grandparents' motorhome and causing everyone a great amount of alarm. Because my greatest fear was to wet the bed I got up in the depth of my dream state, climbed down the ladder, said something to my grandmother who was sleeping below, walked back to the bathroom, took care of business, and then continued to carry on a conversation (that evidently made little sense), and then climbed back up to the bunk and slept until morning. To hear my grandmother tell the tale you would have thought I had a mental illness, but that was pretty much how I passed through life, or at least how I envisioned it felt like for everyone around me. I wet the bed, walked in my sleep, and didn't make much sense.

Social awkwardness comes with growing up. Had someone told me this I might have handled it better. Instead it was just another layer of confusion that made me feel constantly out of place, out of time, out of sync with the rest of reality. I will admit, I was not like the other kids.

I was raised on Monty Python and Dr. Demento. Things were a bit corny in my world and there is a certain amount of wit that comes with British humor that some people just don't get. I remember the last time I laughed out loud in a group of my peers. It was in Junior High and someone had said something that if taken literally was really quite funny. Everyone turned to look at me as I stood at my locker laughing. That was the last time I let myself laugh until recently.

Tempering your reactions to life to appease the crowd becomes endless. There is no way to know what people are going to find funny, offensive, or downright weird. I had come to the conclusion that my mind was just different. There were lots of dialogs running at any given time; lots of debates and quandaries. I loved to learn. I loved to read, to write, to play teacher and assign everyone homework. More than those things I liked to wonder; to think about why things happened the way they did, how the birds stayed in the air even as the wind pummeled their tiny frames, how a child could actually someday become an adult. The great mysteries.

In my thinking, everything was knowable if you just knew where to look for the answers. I loved the Encyclopedia Britannica and the Unabridged Dictionary that accompanied them. It must have been six inches across at the spine! They have all the cuss words in there you know. It was a great place to find the meaning of things and discover all that the adult world wanted me to know nothing about. I learned much in those pages and began to better understand the world I lived in. I also learned that there was one less compound word in my dictionary than in Aaron Canter's when he beat me out of the class competition in third grade. I was convinced he cheated somehow. There was no doubt in my mind that my intellect and vocabulary eclipsed my peers. I mean, they didn't get me. I was weird.

Knowledge and understanding sound the same, but could be no different than night and day. I "knew" a lot of things. I did not "understand" much of anything, or at least anything that mattered. I knew life was not what it appeared, that there were questions I had no answers for, and something deep inside was not right, but I did not understand any of it. It was a lingering feeling, that like all the other feelings, I put out to pasture and hoped maybe a rogue coyote would eliminate it so I would not have to tend to it in the future.

Most of life makes little to no sense in the moment and that serves us pretty good until we get further down the road and realize that everything that came before has some bearing on where we are today.

The moment we look over and realize the objects in the mirror are closer than they appear, we are forced to take a deeper look; to stare history in the face and take hold of all the things we thought we buried along the roadside.

Some people are trash haulers. They carry a heavy load dragging it behind them everywhere they go and like to talk about their struggles and problems to anyone with ears. I was more of an undertaker. I liked to bury things... deep, like forty or fifty feet below sea level. Now, for future reference, just be aware that tying weights onto your feelings and problems and throwing them overboard is not very effective. At first they will sink, but eventually either the water level drops and exposes the debris or the pesky little escape artists find their way to the surface. They have a life of their own and they don't like to be neglected or forgotten either, and they will tell you about it when they find you. And trust me they will find you. After all, they live in you.

There is no way to escape what lives inside of you. You can do your best to kill them off or silence the screams, but they will always haunt you, reminding you that they were (and are) real, alive, and powerful. They may not always feel like part of you, but they are you. Stranger still, they are quiet foes who seem to be trying to protect you from more emotional damage, but mostly just cause more trouble than they are worth as they mask the pain and memories. And that is the crazy thing about memories, they are remembered--again and again and again.

Memories are like a faucet -- if it remains off there is no water, no flood, no disaster. It is pretty uninteresting. But turn it on, even just a little, and the seemingly insignificant drops will soon become a tiny puddle. Open the valve more and you will have a situation on your hands, especially if you had not planned on anything flowing out when you turned the knob. And once that mess forms you quickly forget how it started. You become so focused on trying to mop up the puddles that you fail to turn off the water. And before long you are floating down a river of your own tears. This was how I found myself... alive but broken... swimming, but mostly drowning. In what, I hardly knew, but life was about to open the floodgates to history and I was afloat with nothing but my tiny water wings of spiritual understanding.

CHAPTER 2

Growing, Wilting, and Gushing Fountains

"Jesus said, 'Everyone who drinks this water will get thirsty again and again. Anyone who drinks the water I give will never thirst--not ever. The water I give will be an artesian spring within, gushing fountains of endless life."

--John 4:13-14 MSG

Gardens and fountains have always felt historical and beautiful and full of life to me. Walking through the gardens of Versailles or the Royal Gardens of Europe was like a giant pause and a deep breath wrapped into one amazingly brilliant package. They were full of fragrance, color, and most of all a place of serenity.

I remember a picture I saw online not too long ago of abandoned gardens and greenhouses. I was taken by the fact that even in their unkempt state, there was still life and an eerie elegance amidst the abandoned remains of what was initially a very beautiful place. It gives me hope that maybe even the worst of situations can be redeemed with the right degree of insight and perseverance.

I have never been much of a gardener, and as I look out the window just now, the trees are all abloom reminding me that even if I don't plant, someone else does. My world is only partly of my making. I don't deny my planting of some of it, but a great deal has either come before me or has been planted without my knowledge. Some are beautiful and others look a lot like weeds.

My life was littered with weeds, some looked pretty from a distance, but most of them contained thorns, bugs, and substances that would leave you itching for days. I was the kid that seemed to fit in everywhere and nowhere all the same. My garden didn't look like everyone else's though I was certain I was doing all the right things. And then the questions began to infiltrate the soil, *maybe I am not a good gardener*, followed by, *maybe I am not a good person.*

I have always loved the colors and array of shapes, but keeping things alive, well... It has always been a struggle. Add to the equation my inattention and as you may expect, there's been a lot of wilting, dying, and guilting going on over the years. Keeping things alive is supposed to be easy. You just add water...

When you add water and fertilizer to weeds you do grow things. Big things. Ugly things. Things that are nearly impossible to remove. And when you finally decide to plant those beautiful flowers, they last for a day or two and then they get choked out by what came before. It is a vicious cycle of life and death and guilt and shame.

Guilt and its partner shame began wrapping their webs around the leaves of my so-called garden. At first there was a deceptive beauty to their designs and a glow with the morning dew that kept me from seeing their wicked ways, yet they too were choking the life out of me.

Until recently shame was just a word, but that insidious beast has been creeping around my garden for a long while. So long that it had replicated about four or five generations of its minions to wreak havoc in my life.

I would love to be able to share that I have one thing I am ashamed of, but then I would most likely have to claim my whole self. Shame took its sticky threads and wove for me a web of lies, of cover ups, of masks to keep others from seeing my own disappointment in myself, and a life of disguises to distance myself from the pain.

Historically, pain isn't something I remember. I remember incidents. I remember injuries. I remember not knowing what to do. But pain, pain seemed to elude me, or so I had convinced myself as I split off into character after character.

When the mind does its magic tricks there often isn't a huge production, but the players do show up and take on their roles. The disappearing act makes things vanish. The bunny magically appears in the hat. The woman in the box gets cut in two and yet somehow survives. It was the splitting, the breaking apart, the lingering feeling that I was missing something that haunted me -- the times when time didn't make sense, when reality didn't seem at all like where I belonged. A circumstance would arise and I would become the person for that situation, much like an actor -- the transition nearly seamless.

Triggers and overwhelming circumstances often happen in secret, in a personal space, not out in the open. And so, as I began to gather my little friends as seasons passed, they too began to tend to the garden

-- each with their own way and ideas of how to amend the soil, prune the branches, or dig out the ugly. To put it bluntly, my life and garden were a shitshow. There was a strange stench rising from somewhere in there and none of my personas had an answer. Out of a crowd of problem solvers, not one could make that smell go away!

So saddled with my guilt and shame and an odorous cloud over my head, I rode away down the path of life, not knowing that my companions were holding me back, dragging me down, and keeping me from growing up. Somewhere in the garden, where the weeds flourished, I was stunted and began to wilt.

Wilting is a process of dying. By this point you probably think I have some preoccupation with death, but actually all this dying does have a point. There takes some amount of dying in order to give rise to the life to come. So just hang in there, we will get to the living part in a bit.

Like I was saying, wilting is a draining of life. I remember as a kid the image in my mind of Jonah sitting there in his rebellion and God giving him shade just to have it all wilt away. In fact, it had fully shriveled up! The water and life were drained out of it. The scorching sun robbed all the moisture from its being. Much like that stalk, with every new stage of life, it felt harder and harder to maintain composure, to look alive, to stand tall and strong. Even as the various personas took the edge off of situations for me, the vessel of me still had to bear the burden of carrying all these protectors.

Now by some people's assessment these protectors were like alternate personalities, and oftentimes they seemed to dictate life outside of the norms of my general state of mind. Whether we are talking about Dissociative Identity Disorder or just an ordered coping with traumatic circumstances and being triggered to respond in kind, you decide. All that I know is that one day, nine different voices came together and there was a sense of completeness and peace that I cannot fully describe to you. All that to say, if my life seems a bit strange and contradictory, these personas may have had something to do with it and why the stress of life seemed constant even on the best of days.

Stress, when worn like a fine garment, becomes burdensome down the road. It was never meant to be worn day in and day out. It was to be an indicator of circumstance, something to identify for a moment and relieve, not a constant showpiece. But what I adorned myself with on the outside, just eroded the peace within. The turmoil of juggling all the pieces, keeping afloat in the tempest, it would all fall one day and sink. Deeper and deeper into the dark caverns of regret until the day I could gently take hold of the personas and relieve each one of their torments, their fears, and their shame.

Shame is a lot like a band of unruly protestors that show up when the circumstances are right. They march and picket, shout and wave their signs until their message is received and acted upon. They send you into the land of regret and remorse, but mostly they rob you and pilfer and destroy your peace. Now take the scene with the one united voice and break it into nine different voices and points of shame and you have a pretty good idea what the dialog in my head was from the time I woke up until I went to sleep everyday. I couldn't escape the shame. I couldn't escape myself. I couldn't calm the voices within. I couldn't grow up.

Growing up, much like plants in a garden, takes a bit of tending to. I would run to the fountain and water my garden, but the relief was temporary at best, and at worst it brought forth things I had not considered.

I was a contemplative child, yet in all my thinking I came to only a handful of conclusions: people couldn't be trusted, God was bigger than me, and I was pretty sure if I wanted to accomplish something determination would deliver.

Now determination without full contemplation of the consequences has the potential to grow some really nasty weeds in your garden. In an effort of self-protection, I planted a carnivorous plant at the entrance and hoped that deterrent would remove any obstacles to my dreams that stood in the way. Its aggressive stance did keep people out, but it also kept me in. What I also didn't realize was that the fountain I was pulling water from was not from an artesian spring, but one with sediment and potential harm to my health and wellbeing. The more I isolated myself in my garden, wrapped in my ambitions and shame, the more I withered, and the less I interacted with reality.

It was reality that made me realize that even as I grew, I was failing to thrive. The more I tried, the more I failed. I could not see that the water was making me weak and I was no more than a child in a growing body; unable to see the reality in front of me, escaping into fantasies and falsities, and unrealities.

Falsity is the essence of being untrue, incorrect, or insincere. I needed untruth to feel normal. I wanted correctness as long as it didn't disrupt my fragile soul. I wanted sincerity more than life itself, but had no idea how to obtain it. Everything seemed like a show, a putting on of faces, and a performance to not be seen for what I knew I was... a shame.

And there in that garden, some of my own making and some planted by others, I began to see the choking truth of shame and the web of lies that would eventually lead me to life again, but not before I allowed others to walk the path through the beds and planters and assess the mess I had become.

CHAPTER 3

Freedom From The Boxes

"God makes a home for the lonely; He leads the prisoners into prosperity, Only the stubborn and rebellious dwell in a parched land."

~PSALM 68:6 AMP

It was a resurrection; the breath of life injected into dry bones, a seed rising through the dense soil longing to breach the surface and soak in the pure radiance of the sun.

It had been a cold winter, much colder than the ones before with a foot of snow and ice and wind. It was like my heart, though I had no idea at the time. Like I said before, death was my existence; it nibbled at me until I was but a scar and a lifeless thing. But there was beauty in the snow, much like I believe now there was still in me as I waded through the inches of white wonder among the weeds and trees.

As I walked in the early morning quiet, the snow crunching underfoot, there was a knowing that this peace, this absence of activity and solace along the river's edge that mesmerized and hypnotized me, was not the end. It felt like a beginning, but of what? It was a mystery.

Mystery has an element of intrigue. It taunts you and beckons you to come closer, poke around a bit, examine things you had ignored before. As the snow melted there was an unsettled feeling that lodged itself in my flesh and wouldn't let go. It was like a fishhook of darkness, the blackness of which was so dense that it threatened to swallow up all light. It was menacing and yet I knew it sought my life, I had to investigate it; take a sharp stick and stab into the void and wait to see what happened. I had nothing to lose, I was pretty much dead anyway.

Feeling dead and being dead, without a pulse and cold, are pretty similar. The absence of feeling, the ambivalence toward everything, the lack of care or concern for another day or even another person--they all add up to death. As I drove across the Sellwood Bridge I knew the minute I thought it, this was the end. The end of what was yet to be determined, but the words came quickly, "I could drive off this bridge and no one would even care." But deep down I knew that wasn't true. Even if no person would have sought me out, I knew God would know, and that alone kept my deathly thoughts from action.

There are few things that I fear more than bears and the wrath of God is one of them. As a child I firmly believed that my every misstep was being recorded in a big book in heaven and God was taking a running inventory of all my sins day to day. When my grandmother died I believed she too was sitting on a cloud reporting to God my misdeeds and failings. I swore (okay, more like an oath) to never swear, to never break the Ten Commandments, to be essentially sinless. This kind of thinking either drives one mad or drives those around them mad. I gave my life to the cause, determined not to fail. I failed -- miserably actually.

It is failing, when one seeks to be self-reliant, that causes perfectly fertile soil to become rife with weeds. Pride, like the serpent it is, slithered past and I was intrigued by its offerings. He spread a few seeds and I watered them. I knew if I just tried hard enough I could be perfect. Sure, no one before me had ever been able to pull it off, but I was determined to be the first even if I had to overlook my own sins.

Being first was somewhat of a game to me. My attentiveness often afforded me a front row seat to life. I always was near the front of the class and would fight to be line leader if for some reason my place was second or third in line. I had issues with Andersons and Barnetts, they were constantly seeking to overthrow my reign. (*The audacity of some people!*) If they only knew my name meant “priceless” and “beyond worth or measure” they would have understood their position in my kingdom. They never did and that infuriated me.

Holding the keys to your own kingdom sounds wonderful and inviting until you discover that there is a loneliness within the castle walls that far outweighs being a servant in the kingdom of another. There is nothing like the coldness that settles in when you are dreadfully alone. And when the blinders come off and you realize it was your own pride and arrogance that established your kingdom, well there is a great amount of guilt. And guilt when you are the master of your universe can only be removed by self-effort and that too fails on many counts.

I hated failure in the worst way. If there was a way to cover my shortcomings I did. My oath to never lie was shattered as my life became more lie than truth. It wasn’t that I wanted to deceive people, I just didn’t want them to know... I was broken. I was hurting. I was human.

The idea of being human is not foreign to most who walk this fine planet, but it wasn't until a few months ago I fully grasped what being human meant and it resulted in an overhaul of my thinking. I guess when you are dead you don't need to address what life form you are, but I had never really thought of myself as human. A person maybe. A homosapien for the sake of classification, but not human. Humans were flawed, broken, imperfect creations that wounded and made errors, they had feelings, and... sinned. I was certainly not one of those, and if I was, I would never admit it. I was strong, self-sufficient, smart, spiritual, athletic, confident that I knew how to live my life, and I was certainly not one to admit imperfection and sinfulness (those were the labels on boxes in the closet). And that was what confronted me on the bridge that day. I was broken. I was a sinner. I was very near my end like everyone else, afraid to face the truth.

I can be a bit of a cynic, which seems a bit ironic given the circumstances. My distrust of humanity was clear -- the world was out to get me, or if not to get me, to obliterate me completely. The best way I knew to shield myself from the masses was to become smart, more specifically smarter than them. I was always on guard ready to thwart the next incoming attack, wielding my wisdom and jabbing with my words, and to my credit I had to fight very little given the height of my wall and my stalwart defenses. I became very adept at self-protection and within my fortress I withdrew to draw up new maps and schemes to keep out the enemy. That is what people were -- the enemy.

Now people are not the true enemy. The enemy that seeks to destroy us may well use people, may even use our own minds against us, but people... they are not the enemy.

Enemies are typically those who want to harm you, they come in the dead of night to conquer your kingdom, tear down the things you have worked so hard to build up. I am sure now that there were never as many enemies pounding down my door as my imagination conjured up, but I was convinced at the time that if I let down the drawbridge and called back the lions and corralled the piranhas swimming in the moat, I would be destroyed.

The problem with fear is that 99.9% of the time it is unfounded. We create scenes in our minds, run through scenarios that will never come to fruition, and make up stories of how our choices will in the end ruin our lives. We spin like tops in our prayer closets and bedrooms begging God to deliver us from something that doesn't even exist and when the scene doesn't change we find ourselves feeling more alone, more abandoned, more forgotten.

Feeling forgotten changes things, and when you feel like God has forgotten you, you believe all sorts of lies like God is the boogeyman crawling out from under the bed to get you and that He only wants to punish and chastise you. For most of my life I didn't understand God. One minute He seemed to be saying He loved me and sent His Son for me and the next He was wagging His finger at me as He pointed to the gates of hell. I never questioned the reality of God or of hell. I was pretty sure I would barely make it into heaven in the end, and spent a lot of time as a kid rehearsing my deathbed confession just to make sure I would make the cut.

I like to think I am a product of a failed euthanasia system. Don't get me wrong, I loved almost everything about church growing up. I had perfect attendance, went to summer camps and retreats, acted in the church plays, and lived in the t-shirt. There was no denying I played the part well and church was a big part of my life. The problem was the system demanded my submission to the code, and as a good perfectionist, I was addicted, and addiction (as we know) typically leads to death.

Addiction comes in a million different forms and nobody thinks much about addiction if it is positive. In fact, most of the time when people see a "healthy" or "positive" addiction they actually encourage you to push harder into the depths of it. I always found addictions, or I stumbled into them, or tripped over them. I am pretty sure nobody thought I was addicted, fanatical, but not addicted.

I was born an evangelist. If there is something I am passionate about you will know about it. I have sold a number of cars that match mine, bicycles, phones, computers, and books to my friends. I could probably have made a good living in sales if I was pushing a product I really believed in, but I hated salespeople. They always seemed fake, snake oil pushers, bent on getting me to buy something I didn't want. Adults seemed that way to me growing up. I believed I wasn't like those people. I was passionate. And passionate people, well, we don't fit into boxes very well. And everyone in this world really has a thing for boxes.

Church was the little white box of a building where we sat quietly, memorized scripture, sang songs out of tune, and drew cartoons on scraps of paper as the minister gave his orations. Much like the tree in my backyard, it was a refuge and a place where I felt like I belonged. There was a predictability to it that I craved, and Sunday school teachers to look up to and impress. I felt connected to something bigger than myself. That was different.

I liked different -- a lot. Normal was boring. There was a resistance that called to me when something was deemed "different"; set apart, curious. I wanted very much to align myself with the unknown. Church was not that place, but Christianity was. Walking through life as a billboard for Jesus was quirky and weird. People never quite knew what to think when you wore your trendy looking t-shirt with the Bible verse cleverly disguised in the design. It made me feel righteous and above the fray. I was just glad no one ever asked me what the verse said or what I believed because I could recite verses I memorized, but could not tell you what any of it meant. I was like a computer filled with data just waiting for a defrag, but unable to arrange the information on my own to create a cohesive understanding. I was like the unbeliever who Jesus spoke to in parables; continually hearing but not understanding, always looking but never seeing.

Blindness, especially spiritual blindness, makes deadness just a little more dead. It is a lot like climbing in a box and waiting, like a jack-in-the-box, for someone to wind you up enough to pop you through the lid and scare the crap out of them. There is a stillness of soul that to call it dormant is to anticipate life to come, but it really seems much more grave and final. When you crawl into that box, whether by your own making or succumbing to life's demands and tortures, there is a deep belief that you are climbing into a coffin. The thought that someone might actually turn the handle or release the latch, well that is mostly just a fantasy. There is no light, no optimism, just the realistic expectation that this is it. It is as good as it gets. So, numb out everything; fear, pain, all of it and just take a long winter's nap.

When Sleeping Beauty comes to life we all knew it would happen. If it didn't Disney would be in trouble and millions of parents would be up in arms. When the average person slips into a state of existing, that spiritual and emotional coma of everyday life, we hardly take notice. We don't expect them to change or even believe that change is possible. That is just the way they are. They're depressed. They're grumpy. They're distant. We rarely stop and think that maybe they just need their prince to come, that the forces of evil are doing everything in their power to keep Sleeping Beauty from the kiss of her prince and taking a long sip of the Water of Life.

The references to “living water” and “water of life” always were good poetry to me, but to know their meaning, well, that took a long walk in the desert to understand. And as I stood there, all my pride dashed on the hard clay, I was thirsty. Thirsty for life, but more so for God.

Water is the most life-giving resource I can think of and it has always drawn me. It is a basic element of life. To try to live without it is foolish and will expedite the dying process. As I sat in the desert of my wandering, in denial of all my sin, I was parched. The sun beat down with a fury I had not known as the buzzards circled overhead. I was not a beauty at this point as I hung in a lucid state of sleep, teetering on the edge of reality as the mirage hovered on the horizon. If only I could crawl a bit further, try a bit harder at this thing called life, then maybe I could find the life everyone always said was available. But my body was tired. I was tired. And though I could see a light rising in the distance, doubt flooded in reminding me of how far I had traveled on my hands and knees and never found anything that had been promised. But I was thirsty -- more thirsty than I ever remember being before. Just to look at a running stream again, to know that the flow of life and energy existed, to watch the ripples and current dance along rock and limb... life. I had to find it. I had to take hold of it, even if it killed me.

To crawl out of the desert takes courage that in that moment you do not realize you are activating. There is a desperation as you feel the claws of death digging into your cooling flesh that summons the last ounce of strength, the final burst of adrenaline, the thought that if this is truly your last breath it would be better to go out in a blaze of glory than to curl up in the fetal position. I landed squarely on the fatalistic thought that if the play was going to come to a close it might as well have a climax or dramatic ending.

Had I known walking out of one scene and into another would profoundly change my life I may have avoided plays for the rest of eternity, but like so many times before I had to choose -- the door on stage right or stage left? Door number one was familiar, known, a box where I had settled for over half my lifetime. Door number two pleaded for me to come, but held uncertainty and questions; questions that if left unanswered would provide even more questions. And that is faith -- walking into the unknown, not because it makes sense or you can wrap your head around it (most likely you never will so trying is a waste of brain activity), but because you know it is what you need to do.

A turbulent spring came to a close with a storm. Storms, or rather upheavals, draw out the best and worst in us. Our minds don't like change; they like order, routine, knowns, formulas. When a storm comes there are no guarantees and predicting the outcome is shoddy at best. So, with faith in hand, we batten down the hatches, brace for the worst, and wait for the shearing winds and pelting rain to pass. It is like a beating of drums, a surging of power, a breaking off. It was tribal and peaceful, and when the pulsing ended, the chords rang out until they faded into the dim morning light of the sunrise. I knew life would never be the same. The box had survived, but it was soaking wet and deteriorating around me. *Was freedom truly available?* I wanted to know.

Freedom sounds amazing until you realize that with freedom comes responsibility. I have the freedom to eat whatever I want, but my body will only cooperate with me if it gets the nutrients it needs to survive. If I feed it Cheetos and Pepsi it will shut down, but if I fill my stomach with nutrient dense food I will thrive. The desert had filled my physical stomach with sand, and the rest of me was left wanting. As I looked out on the vast horizon, my calloused knees dry from the desert, I could taste the goodness. I took in its scent, only it wasn't the scent, more like the flavor -- like a strange foreign spice that you roll around your mouth that feels like a smooth marble that you don't want to swallow. You long to savor it.

I am not one to linger too long. I enjoy long walks on the beach or in the forest, but I don't sit still for any amount of time. You know you have stumbled on something magnificent when you stop and feel like you just can't take it all in. Falls Creek Falls at the height of the Autumn runoff does that for me. I could stand there and watch the water pound down for hours. You almost have to pull me away. I get so wrapped up in it. And that is how you know you have found what you are looking for; you can't move, you can't speak, you know it is beautiful and yet it could kill you instantly, you feel the power and rumble beneath your feet and in it is a peace that doesn't make sense. That is how you know how small you really are, and that humbling is the beginning of understanding. The beginning of life.

Humility has a way of sneaking up on you. It isn't something that you can try harder to be or predict when it will come. It is more disturbing than that. If it is pride that causes us to hide in boxes and disguise our blemishes, then it is humility that says it is okay to come outside; to dare to be seen.

It was the white box, the sandbox, and all the other boxes I tried to fit in that drove me to a dead stop. It was awe that awoke me from my sleep. And that was it. Death stopped. I threw open the lid to the first box to find the next one, and like a stack of Russian nesting dolls I slowly emerged; each flap rising higher than the last and a little more light shining in reminding me that I was still a viable seed. I had been hidden in storage, but the rains were coming and the sun would bring life to my dormant soul once again.

CHAPTER 4

Open Doors and Empty Closets

"For You have rescued my soul from death, Yes, and my feet from stumbling, So that I may walk before God In the light of life."

~PSALM 56:13 AMP

When blind eyes get their first glimpse of light the immediate response is to cover them back up. The light is too bright. There is too much to take in all at once and yet the rest of the world does it everyday. It isn't that the light is extraordinarily radiant. It isn't that they can't see. They have been healed of that ailment. The problem lies in the penetrating nature of light.

Light and darkness, truth and lie, the goodness of God and the badness of me, they are all made known when the Truth shines in. Just a shimmer of light brings truth into the darkest of caves. It is in that place of being found that two decisions stand before you: dig deeper into the darkness, or throw your hands up and walk out into the light.

Walking out of hiding, like a thief caught red-handed, was what I feared most. It was the public confession of my sins as I raised my hands in surrender and came forth unarmed, or disarmed, or just humbled with the reality that I was never very good at defending myself in the first place. As I quaked under the weight of the unknown, I gave myself to Truth. I was done with the lies.

Lies are like tiny snares meant to trap and entangle us, not necessarily to kill us. The hunter hunts, but the traps are laid and left for the prey to wander into them, and most who find themselves entrapped usually don't die until they struggle to get free. And that was the fear. *If I tried to lose myself would I bleed out?*

Bleeding, like so many other things, always left me feeling alone. I remembered as a child skinning my knee, cutting my finger, or finding a sliver buried deep within my flesh and making my way into the bathroom to find the necessary tools to doctor myself up. I am not sure one way or the other if anyone would have helped, but I certainly wasn't about to confess my distress, and so I took care of myself. The pattern repeated when puberty finally hit. I figured life out. That was how it was, but it intensified my independence in a way that would fuel my pride and leave humility at the wayside... or in the closet of neglect and pain.

As a child I spent a lot of time in my closet. It was a safe place to hide away where no one seemed to bother me and I could sit with a flashlight behind a layer of clothes and write in my diary all the things I wanted to happen in my life. I would write in code the deepest desires and secrets of my heart with a shred of hope that maybe I would someday know them in truth. They were my own little fantasy that I hoped would come to fruition, but as I sat there one night I questioned every bit of it. I could hear the voices in the hall, and then in a flash, the closet door swung open and I was greeted with the demand to know, "Are you on drugs or something?!" And when my sheepish answer was "no" they seemed to not believe me.

Now you must understand, I was the kid who never swore, never ran with the wrong crowd, and begged to go to church activities. If there were drugs at school I wouldn't know the first thing about finding them. I hardly knew what a joint was, and that was only because I was in the "Just Say No" club. The irony of having parents that accuse you when you have never done anything wrong is like trying to get milk from a bicycle. You can try all you want, but what you are looking for won't be there. But because my life was a mystery to everyone I was always left in the camp of the untrusted, and when you feel like no one believes you you begin to wonder if maybe you really can't be trusted. Maybe the answer is to climb further into the closet. Maybe it is to disappear completely.

Disappearing and hiding in boxes and closets is a temporary solution to a lifetime of problems. The more boxes you stuff full and stash away, the more times you climb in and make a nest in the corner, the greater the disaster to come. You see, a closet has limited space and at some point it hits capacity. When the doors start to bow and there is no longer a place for you to nest down inside, you lean against the doors from the outside fearful that it will all come tumbling out. We can spend years leaning on those doors, stuffing whatever little hurts and sins we can under the door until the day it can be held back no longer.

When we finally lean forward, away from protecting our "treasure", and reach for the promises of God we have a momentary lapse of memory. We forget why we were sitting there holding the door. But moving forward just that inch reminds us in an instant. We have hid a lot in that closet. And as the boxes shift and the door opens, everything (Every. Single. Thing.) falls out on the floor and we come face to face with all of the pain, all of the secrets, all of the sins and brokenness. We are seen. Seen in all our naked truth. Every little bit out in the open.

I could not have anticipated that one offense, one jolt to my system, one more hurt would fling open the closet door and lay me bare, but it did. And as I laid there in the piles and piles of life there was a knowing that nothing, absolutely nothing, would be the same again.

There comes a moment in our undoing when we stop being shocked by our nakedness, when we look up to see that God isn't mortified by our flesh, that He is not ashamed of us, just sad that it took us so long to come to this point. He has waited a lifetime to see us unveiled, undone, and exposed under the light of His truth.

Exposure is a frightening thing. *What if I am not seen as lovely? What if the truth is worse than I thought? What if there is no grace on the other side?* It begs questions that in the end question the very nature of God.

Growing up with the idea of God as the great and mighty judge left me with very little understanding of His love. To wrap my mind around a love that was not based on my ability to pay off my debt or sinfulness made no sense. God obviously wanted and deserved my penance.

When the blinders come off, and you take in His brilliance, a lot of things are confusing and the question "why" circles about like a shark in shallow waters. As I waded into the waters along the salty shoreline the fin stayed in my line of sight. I needed to know the meaning, but feared moving in too close. If love really was free, if grace was truly unmerited, well... this could be the greatest thing ever. If none of those things were true, my seeking would only lead to further injury. But there was a draw; a compulsion stronger than the most intense electromagnetic field pulling me closer, calling my name, asking me to trust.

Trust when you have very little history doing such a thing is uniquely distressing. In fact, it is almost incomprehensible. So when God began to speak to my heart in four simple words, "Do you trust Me?" I scarcely knew what to reply, but I found myself repeatedly just saying "Yes", almost as if no other answer existed.

When You finally look up and into the eyes of Jesus, you know. There is just something in the smile as the tears well up in His eyes. He doesn't have to say a word. You just know. And the love you feel, it compels you to take it in, accept it in its entirety, denying not one bit of it. The question of trust dissolves under the warming touch of grace and the caress of infinite love. The English language fails me when I seek out the words to describe the intensity of being known and loved. You could try to equate it to human relationships, but that somehow seems to cheapen it.

There is not a relationship between humans that can even come close to what transpires between the Creator and His creation. The intimacy goes beyond the revealing and exposure to fulfilling the most obscure of wants and desires. No human can complete us, but God certainly can, and does. There is not one molecule that He doesn't know every detail of, and that is precisely why His love can't be quantified or comprehended for all it is. The Creator of absolutely everything, every part of me down to the smallest of details, created in me the desires exactly as He saw fit and longs to fulfill those things in me. It is so unlike earthly relationships where we hunt around in the lives of others hoping to find, or have them reveal, the person they are within. God already knows, and He comes ready to make our every need complete in Him.

I sought completeness in other people for most of my life only to come up more incomplete the further down the road I went. I was like a jigsaw puzzle, constantly gathering pieces in hopes of finding out what the picture of me looked like. I had no idea that all the random pieces I took from the lives of others would not complete me. I gathered more and more scraps of what I thought I needed, amassing more hurt, more pain, and more fragmentation within my own already damaged soul. What I needed was God, but I felt so unworthy, so incapable of approaching Him in the state I was in. But to be complete would be to become one within myself and one with Him; to have His Spirit reside in me, to fill me, to quell the yearning of my heart.

The idea of love completing me always seemed mushy, like mash potatoes and gravy or chocolate cake with sprinkles. The God I knew was staunch and intellectual, reasonable, but more like Michelangelo's depiction of God in the Sistine Chapel. There was sternness to Him, not a warm cuddly man, or a Father. I never could call Him Father, and certainly not Papa. He was Lord. He was God; big, ominous, demanding of my obedience. I was small, dirty, and unworthy.

The day I realized that there was no washroom en route to His presence I was dumbfounded. I remembered the lessons of my childhood, the ones where my Sunday school teacher would explain the Temple, the outer courts, and the Holy of Holies. How the priest would have a rope tied around his ankle as he entered the sacred place of God's presence just in case he "didn't make it". That was the God I knew, full of judgment and wrath, no one explained clearly that God wasn't like that anymore. His Son changed all that.

God never asks us to wash our face and clean up before we come to Him. I guess that is mostly because if we could scrub ourselves clean we would have no need for Him. So He stands, with a wet rag in hand, waiting for our tired and muddy souls to realize we need to be made clean. All our efforts to wash away the dirt and alleviate our suffering are not enough. And though we come with a foul odor and cloaked in layers of all the ungodliness of life, He receives us and He loves us anyway. It is unbelievably wonderful. Awesome. Profound really.

Profundity takes a thought, drives about a mile beyond what we can perceive, shape shifts into yet something absolutely outside of our realm of creativity, and then boomerangs back to us with an effectiveness in the area of our need with the precision that rivals the most skilled of engineers. And that is God. Profoundly wonderful at meeting our every expectation in ways that our minds cannot even begin to comprehend. And the price of this profound gift of God... of love? It is nothing more than surrender to His Spirit and walking into all truth. It is His Spirit and His truth that call for us to reciprocate with the reality of who we are. The result: we live, we become real.

Being real and wanting to be real compete for our attention. It is a lot like the Velveteen Rabbit. How does one become "real"? One must allow themselves to be loved. Loved to the point where your fur gets rubbed off and your eyes come out. You find humility in knowing that the sacrifice that looks like death is what will bring you life. The more you let Him love you, the more you live. The more you live, the more you enjoy the feast that God places before you day in and day out.

Though there is a great banquet in the presence of God, intimacy with God is not like eating, more like dancing and twirling and acting silly. It isn't that it is undignified, but it doesn't always make a whole lot of sense. It isn't linear, or something we can predict or calculate. It is kind of like celery, it seems like a non-food until you realize how much fiber is in it and how it will keep you regular. It may not be like eating, but it feeds the soul in a way other things don't.

Worship has a way of quenching the thirsty soul. As I wandered out of the desert I was greeted in the most unexpected way and asked to lead worship at a church that was new to me and yet vaguely familiar. It felt like redemption; like grace. It was as if every mis-step had been ignored and I was being released back into the life I had run from long ago when it had all become too hard and threatened to awaken my slumbering emotions, though this time I would not run. I wanted to feel. I wanted to be real. I wanted to live... to love.

Wanting to live and understanding what that entails are two different things. One can want to live and lay there waiting for others to pick them up or you can put on your running shoes and go. I strapped on my seatbelt, put the car in gear, and hit the accelerator. I had years to make up for; years that I was sure I would be paying for at some point, but years I wanted to make up for more than anything else. I felt the guilt and shame. I could not live one more moment of wandering, or sleeping, or dying. I had been called and He was asking me to worship openly before everyone -- something I had not done in so many years I hardly remembered what it was like or how to go about it. My long-time friend assured me it was like riding a bike, so I climbed on and secured my feet on the pedals.

For months I had not been able to shake from my mind a certain list of songs. It had made me feel uncomfortable to a point. Why would God be asking me to take my first opportunity to lead worship in years and give me a complete set that at best I could only intellectually understand, and at worst could ruin me? It plagued me like the fear of the villagers before Saint Patrick escorted the snakes from Ireland, though that too was a fairytale. But I knew, truer than the blue of the sky, this was exactly what God was asking of me.

Music has always gripped me in a way that nothing else has quite been able to rival. A melody, a simple poetic line, held the ability to captivate my mind for hours. Some might say it has always been an idol, that perfect piece of art that I would stare endlessly toward, and believe someday it would deliver to me the fullness I was convinced it held for my soul. There was an energy, an aliveness, that music always brought me. It was, at times, the only reason I knew I was alive. Those fleeting moments when I felt, truly sensed, a waking -- an opening in the window of my heart.

To feel was foreign, like answering the phone and hearing a voice in a language that sounded more like gibberish than actual words. In the months since crawling out of the arid wasteland I had felt the stirring.

I was beginning to undergo a change. I was enduring an upheaval of things, not anything I could wrap words around. Confusing waves that went unidentified. They were fabulous and horrible all at once. I would later come to realize they were emotions; true human, legitimate emotions. I would be walking along and find myself smiling and laughing for no reason! I would hear words and the fires of anger and frustration would rise up. It was wild and new and out of control. I loved it. I hated it.

When life comes to a crossroads and you pick a road with no idea what lies ahead, there is an element of adventure that fills you with adrenaline and gives you hope. It isn't that you disbelieved the brochures about the Promised Land, but you hope (gamble really) that nothing can be as bad as from where you have come. What you don't realize when you set foot out of the desert of certain death is that you *will* be seen. I was naked and God had placed me front and center.

Being naked, goes without saying, is the opposite of being clothed. There is a vulnerability that says nothing, not one speck, is hidden. It is a frightening thing to be naked; to be known.

I liked to be hidden, like Adam and Eve behind their fig leaves. And somehow in my naiveté I actually thought my efforts at concealment did the job to block God's view of my sin. I sewed my fig leaves and pranced about the garden, my shame in full view. I remember the moment it hit me, like a dump truck carrying a load of cement blocks, I was crushed under the realization God knew. He knew it all, from beginning to end. Not just that, but He loved me. To think that I could cover over what He already saw, already knew from the beginning of time... I had been found out before I knew I was lost. He had been pursuing me despite my grossness and ungodly behavior. It blew my mind. It distorted my reality. It forced me to acknowledge something had been missing.

When you give birth you rarely have the pleasure of telling it when to start and when to stop. It, life, decides when to come, how hard or how easy the labor will be, if it is a boy or a girl. And that is just how it was. I honestly had no clue that I was pregnant with this new life. It was kind of like those women on the late night news programs who shock us all when they say they had no idea they were pregnant; their bodies had not given them any signs until the moment they were giving birth. That was how it was. Sudden. Frightening.

Most people, when they talk about finding God they never knew Him. I very much thought I knew Him. I had been to every church camp, baptized in the frigid waters off the Oregon Coast, spent four years at Bible college. My mind was full, but my heart was half empty; half known. It wasn't that He didn't know me, He did. It was that I would not allow myself to be known *by Him* -- not fully anyway. But as I ran through the songs of the worship set, that list that tormented me as my hands fumbled across the fretboard of my guitar, I found myself unable to maintain my composure. I wept. I stopped playing. I fell to the floor and could do nothing more than lay there in awe of grace and cloaked in a love that I had not known.

The waking, the euphoric moment of being found. It was truly like the heavens opened up and poured forth their wonder. Everything stood in perfect order before me; crisp and in focus. This is what they had talked about. This was the elusive clarity of being known; of being loved. It would be a while before the rollercoaster would stop rising and falling, but with each dip, I now held hope and knew a part of me *was* lovable.

I was standing face to face with the God of the universe, the Creator of all things, and He wasn't mad or threatening, He was strong and mighty, but incredibly loving. More loving, in fact, than I ever thought possible. He wasn't pointing out my flaws, He was cheering me on. He wasn't scowling at my failures, He was glowing with pride, as if I was truly the apple of His eye. The moment I had feared, the reckoning as the prodigal returned, was just like in the story (though I had invested years of doubt believing it could never really be). And in an instant I knew, this was love. Not the love that was earned, but unconditional, grace infused, bona-fide love.

Love when you taste it for the first time is a strange fruit. It is sweet and inviting, its aroma alluring, and yet it can barely be described with words. As I laid there unable to speak a single word, my heart leapt inside me with the fullness of a banquet feast. The hole I had spent a lifetime attempting to fill was overflowing. Running over. Taking over. I laid there for what seemed like an eternity, the tears cascading one after another like a waterfall of gratitude. I deserved none of this. I deserved to be beat and left to die a lonely death. I should still be in the desert, yet instead of dying He was pouring new life into me. Glorious, fullness of life.

I would have gladly stopped the love fest at this level of engagement and been satisfied for the rest of my life, but God had another plan.

Just days later, when the Lord began to write His love songs to me, through me, it was almost too much to take. Unlike so many of my more moody chord choices or overly poetic phrases, these songs were simple, fun, they made me want to put on a sun dress and twirl out in a field somewhere.

Music has always been a good friend to me. I grew up in the era of the mixtape and I would spend hours waiting for the perfect song to come on the radio so I could dub it into the mix. Yes, I was a music pirate before the internet. I stole a lot of things as a kid. And as much as the guilt hit me when I was found out, I had a bit of a compulsion and what I liked to think of as a "need" when it came to purchasing candy, soda, and music (three things a dollar's worth of allowance a week wasn't going to cover). I could never imagine my world without music and money was not going to keep me from the purest expressions I knew and could relate to.

There is something that music does deep down that adds an extra measure, an extra rhythm, a harmonious melody to the song of our heart. It is like you can't help but sing along. It moves us in ways other sounds don't. It can take us to a point of time in an instant, pull us out of a funk, or put us into one. There is power in those chord progressions and arpeggios, those words and expressions. They would sing me to sleep at night and wake me in the morning. So when I asked to play piano and was denied, a part of me sat empty. Then in fifth grade I would get the opportunity to play clarinet in band, though I wanted to play saxophone. Every morning I debated getting sick on the band bus just to avoid the scoldings I received from our conductor when I played by ear rather than reading the sheet music.

Fifth grade held a number of elements that set life apart. The beginning of the year started in traumatic fashion, though I couldn't remember why until just this year, and ended with a whirlwind tour of Southern California theme parks. In between was like one long panic attack. I couldn't think straight. Where once I was a straight "A" student and Math T.A.G. participant, I couldn't even do flash cards as the anxiety took over my mind. I empathized with the chinchilla in the back of our classroom every time the kids made him a nervous wreck and he bit off another of his toes. I longed to take him home and rescue him as well as myself from the madness, but my mother said "no" to being the weekend caretaker. I was empty. I beat myself up for my lack of performance. Accused my teacher of not liking me and that was why I was doing poorly. I knew it was me. I was pretty sure I was dying. Nothing made sense. I know now it was what they call "trauma brain".

I kept my struggle of cognition to myself, determined to unscramble all the signals in my brain and get back to "normal" before I started to be punished for my grades slipping. My mother had bought the story that Mrs. B had it out for me, and by some great miracle I found sanity by year's end, but things were different. I was not the same. There was a new drive to be athletic and strong. And the part of me that was always driven to succeed now had another fear -- losing the ability to achieve. I doubled down on everything educational available to me, and made a simple request to play soccer only to be told, "We are not doing sports on Sunday and I am not going to stand around in the cold and rain!"

It needs to be noted that when it came to interests, hobbies, and things people do for fun, my family was hard to pin down. They listened to music, but didn't play music. They watched football and baseball games (and later basketball only because I would study every game and not allow the channel to be turned), but were never athletic. It was very much like I was dropped from a spaceship or the stork got the wrong house when I was born. Everything I was interested in was like a foreign language to them -- frivolous endeavors. So I escaped into books and blocked out the world with my Walkman. The characters in the pages and the hearts in the songs... they knew me.

Songs are as unique as the people who write them. Every line is a reflection of a feeling or experience conveyed with the backdrop of sound and intensity. As a songwriter I know fully the intoxicating effect of a well written song. I have had the pleasure of writing maybe one such song, but that song when it comes out... it doesn't leave you. So when God began His dance with my heart, singing His song over me, the words and music moved me maybe more than it would most. God knew my language. He knew just how to get to the deepest, most tender part of me. In the late night hours I would take in His song and in the morning I would lay there taking in His sweet melody in the early light of day.

Waking up to a new reality catches you off guard. To say that new life is rebirth is nothing closer than the truth. Every thought, every paradigm, shifts. Things were still messy inside, but there was a strange peace there as well. What was once a world of question marks and fear suddenly had meaning and peace. It isn't that suddenly everything is made right or in order, but everything just makes sense;

there is a purpose, an underlying reason for everything even if the mechanics of it are still kept secret. There's peace. A peace that surpasses understanding and hangs out with friends like love.

I liked my new friends; peace, joy, and love. But like any good friends, they are not about to let you get away without addressing your issues, and I had a lot of issues even as God began to do His work in my heart and life. And as I lay there on the floor, file boxes filled with the documentation of my life pouring over, and the contents of my closet strewn all around me, I could not disbelieve the verity of my mayhem and all that I had tried to obscure behind doors and within closets and in the far depths of my memory. The closet lay empty and I was being made known.

CHAPTER 5

The Unending Circle

"The Lord protects the simple (childlike); I was brought low [humbled and discouraged], and He saved me. Return to your rest, O my soul, For the Lord has dealt bountifully with you. For You have rescued my life from death, My eyes from tears, And my feet from stumbling and falling. I will walk [in submissive wonder] before the Lord in the land of the living."

~PSALM 116:6-9 AMP

How do you stop a problem like Maria? You can't kick her out of the convent, though you would really like to. She is disruptive, unconventional, childish, and has the potential to drag everyone along with her down the road to chaos.

I understood that I was different. How different was a matter of opinion. The rise of emotions in the previous months had brought with it a new power of expression. That power, unharnessed, was like a wild stallion racing across the plains. There was no telling what it was capable of -- it held the strength to build up, but just as much power to destroy. At that moment my "freedom" was threatening to devour every vestige of peace and unravel the cord that had haphazardly bound a church together.

There is a wildness to freedom that when left untamed, runs wild and free and careless. As long as pride fueled me, I was a danger; a bomb waiting to explode, a dam on the verge of collapse. As the waters of unrest stirred in my soul, I cried out to God to bring resolution, but I refused to be put in a box like before.

The fear of being boxed in is a visceral reaction that comes from past oppression. Climbing out of the box takes bravery and courage, and once you get out of the box you come to a new place of freedom, but that freedom requires surrender -- the relinquishing of oneself when you come face to face with your humanity. There is the demand that you must let go of the fear that reminds you of the past entrapment and trust is the only option left on the table. Trust takes surrender and surrender requires humility. It is no wonder pride holds such strength.

It is what keeps us in self-protection and defensive mode once the war is over. It stands as the guard of our heart disallowing anyone to enter. But when we finally hit our end and pride is recognized as foe and not friend and God is welcomed in that you discover that your prayers will be answered, not in the ways you expected, but in the way God so desired to move.

When you ask God for something, what I have found is that you should be really specific. If you ask Him general things you typically don't get an answer. You ask Him to move or change things and often He will do the unexpected. I have come to understand that is just how He is. I am okay with that, but really, someone should have written that in the manual. God doesn’t really care what my comfort looks or feels like, He is way more concerned for my soul and what it will take to change my heart to reflect His. He is the most selfless selfish person I know.

It was that part about God I really didn't like growing up. You know, the part where He created everything to worship Him. It seemed so self-serving and egotistical. If He truly loved us, why would He make us to serve Him, to grovel and beg for forgiveness, only to earn the privilege of worshipping Him for the rest of our lives? It didn't seem like something a loving God would do. It rubbed me wrong.

Love, when you don't understand love, looks a lot like hate. Not hate in the “I want to kill you” sense, but in the “I want to take you captive and enslave you” sort of way. It is uninviting in a way much else is. I never understood why one would freely choose to love or to be loved when it was inevitable -- you would be hurt by it. Love seemed selfish, like I love you so I feel good about me so you feel good about you. It was that circular thing that was really good until it wasn't. I feared the break in the circle more than the circle itself.

Circles are amazing, they link what would be a simple line end to end, completing the whole. Completely endless. It is fascinating to think that no matter how small the circle, it is in fact, endless. And that is love -- one long line with me on one end and God on the other drawn together to form one continuous ring.

To say I understand love is a misnomer. I cannot understand something which resides so far from what words can adequately describe, but I do know what it isn't... pride. Love is not self-seeking. The picture I had held of a God demanding my obedience and reverence held no weight the moment I realized love was a circle; it fueled me and I fueled it. There was an equal measure and yet more coming in than I thought I could handle and more flowing out than I ever thought I was capable of giving.

Love really is a relationship. There is give and there is take, but there is never emptiness or barrenness or lack. Love does not fail. It does not boast. It's not jealous. It's not self-seeking. It's not rude or provoked. It doesn't take into account the wrongs done against it. It bears all things, believes all things, hopes in the worst of times, and endures the unrelenting hardships of life with a steadfastness that makes us wonder if it is legitimately a reality. It is much like looking out over the Promised Land and then walking into it.

The Promised Land was where I thought I had landed as I proudly led worship. I had received a new understanding of God's love, felt a freedom in worship that went beyond anything that had come before, and I thought I was connecting with people. It was true, people were responding to my vulnerability in worship, but once off the stage I held everyone at a distance. I had to. They would never accept the story just under the surface. There was a wholehearted belief that bearing my heart to God before people was the ultimate exposure, but I failed to see that by not connecting on a personal level I was essentially just giving, yet another, performance -- covering my truth in twenty minute displays of spiritual awakening. I was connecting with God, but failing to connect with the community.

People have always been hard for me. I have always been drawn to the human condition and have loved the times when I could make a difference to those emotionally struggling, but the truth was, most of the time I used their traumas to cover my own. It was great that they trusted me, but I could never share the things of my heart with another as they did. My therapists were animals, nature, and books.

I would rather hang out with animals all day than to have to deal with my own kind. All my wounds had a face, a name, a voice. It made interactions uncomfortable and the life of a hermit more inviting. People hurt people. Broken people break people. You just never know what kind of person you are really dealing with until you find yourself wounded. And in all honesty, I was pretty sure the elusive "good person" didn't exist until I set out on this journey.

"Good people" when you find them are just different. You can't help but be drawn to their goodness, yet it seems too good to be true when trust has always resulted in hurt no matter how innocent the face.

Some people are "good" in show only, but the truly radiant ones, well, they are the real deal. A diamond in the rough.

Diamonds come by the application of pressure over time. They don't come out of the ground pretty, but you know when you stumble upon one that it holds the potential to reflect light unlike other rocks. Give it to a master craftsman and that chunk of rock, through cleaving and a keen eye, becomes something wondrous. I don't know a lot about diamonds, but I do know the process of cleaving will literally make or break its value and usefulness. The triangular, octahedral planes mean that four choices in direction are presented to you at each cut. Some diamond roughs are studied for years before the first cleave. And that is how God works -- meticulously.

The most radiant people in my world have all been cleaved and honed by God on the broken road of life. Pulled from the wreckage not much more than a pressurized lump of coal, the Lord examined the complexities and waited for just the right moment, located the apex and tapped -- shearing away the excess and revealing a more brilliant sparkle. Every cut, every shedding, more radiance. And that is how God makes beauty from ashes. He gently taps us in just the right place, breaks off things we didn't necessarily think were bad, and reveals something greater. In the end you find a person who understands what it means to struggle, to fail, and who holds a personal testimony of grace and love. They know intimately their Creator and Sustainer.

I will admit it, I tried really hard to cut diamonds out of stones. I would recognize potential in those around me and then work overtime chipping away at them, always wondering why they never turned out quite right. Sometimes I even did more harm than good. What I didn't appreciate was the work of a master. If I knew a little of something, I knew a lot of something, and I would apply my limited knowledge to coach you to a new level. My heart was to make every sinner a saint, but when it comes to people and character, the only one unequivocally qualified for such a task is God.

Now, every human on the face of the earth holds the power to wound or to heal. God created us in His image, and He is the greatest Physician there is, but He also promises His judgment in the end to those who don't believe. It stands to reason that inside each of us is the ability to be that elusive "good person", if only we were to submit ourselves to the work of the Spirit and let the goodness of God flow through us.

The Spirit, when allowed control of our lives, does unusual things. The "Wild Goose" cannot be caged. My time in Ireland and Wales taught me a lot about the unpredictable nature of the Spirit and the order that to us seems utterly disorganized. Walking the paths of the Welsh Revival years ago made clear to my mind that God will do what He needs to do to move on those He needs to reach. The Celtic people understood you could not domesticate or tame God, that His Spirit would do as He saw fit for the betterment of His people. It is personal, but it is for the whole. It is internal, but it intensely corporate.

It should have come as no surprise to me that the more I submitted my will to His Spirit, the more He would desire to heal me and bring greater healing to the community I was serving. But I was surprised, in the best and worst way. Sitting among other leaders, in an office barely large enough for us all to have a chair, the bomb was dropped into the middle of our circle. Mouths dropped open, damage control began, and I sat reticent. I was fired. It was betrayal.

When the word betrayal pops up in my story it is almost always tied to a woman, which statistically makes sense seeing how I spent a lifetime seeking out big sisters and mothers to fill the emptiness within. The cycle of craving the attention of women capable of leading and mentoring me had led me into many a broken way; where I gave my heart and trust to someone who could never fill the role that was abandoned long before. I gave my heart and my body, hoping, praying that I could feel whole; feel loved. I bounced from mentor to mentor, mother figure to mother figure, and one day settled down in a same sex relationship hoping to find wholeness. Deep down I sought their approval, begged for their love, and longed to be held. I was but a small child trapped in an adult body, seeking endlessly to be given a second childhood filled with everything I felt I had lacked. Most never knew how high I had placed them on the pedestal until the day they were knocked off and the full fury of my rage resulted in an endless silent treatment. I set every woman up to fail, and when they finally displayed their humanness (or lack of support for me), the betrayal stung like walking into a swarm of killer bees.

So, had not the words of my dismissal come from the mouth of the new pastor's wife, I am not sure my reaction would have been as strong. It pierced like a sword through my heart, and confusion wafted through the air like the pungent odor of a skunk.

Skunks can be cute unless you make them upset or threaten them, and their smell lingers long after they leave. In the month leading up to the meeting I had put on my best leader, musician, and tough girl face and set out to conquer every obstacle before me. I needed to prove my prowess. I had made open threats that to thwart me would be messy, but how the mess would play out stunned me and everyone else. With a handful of words and dismissal from my worship leading role, I was disarmed.

Finding oneself disarmed in the midst of battle screams of defeat, and that was very much what it felt like. What stirred within me was not anger or the desperation of retaining one's life in the face of death. I wasn't grieving the loss of my newfound freedom in worship. I was broken, laid out bare, and a great new chapter flipped open in my book.

The pages in my book have a half dozen worn out chapters, a few pages that I have glued together for security reasons, another dozen or so stories that had, up to that point, dictated my every move; drawing me back into circles, not of love and knots and ropes, but the circling time and time again into those deja vu experiences that made my life feel more like the movie Groundhog Day than a continuous journey.

Circles, knots, and the reoccurring scenes of life past in the present were exactly what was on God's heart, and as I retreated to my big empty house and sat down in the middle of my room on the floor, the silence felt like a suffocating pillow. My chest grew tight, my mind could not think, and there in my aloneness the Lord had my full attention.

It is easy to run, to get distracted and not hear the voice of God when He speaks, but when you are disarmed you will do anything to know you will not die in that moment. I pleaded for an answer to the "why". *Why would You (God) give me my heart's desire, only to pull the rug out from under me just as I was taking hold of it?* I wasn't angry. I wasn't mad that my title would be no more. I just wanted to know "why?". And those four words came once again, "Do you trust Me?" And in a violent wave of tears the picture flashed before my mind's eye.

I am a very visual person. To say that I don't live a secondary reality in my mind would probably be somewhat deceptive. Every word, every conversation, every sound and color triggers things in my mind. Whether the things I see in my mind's eye are just my creativity or subconscious or spiritual visions I really can't say, but the reality is that I see things. Not dead people or anything weird like that, but you get the idea. So when God answered my response of "yes" to the trust question with a mind movie, I watched and took it all in.

And so began my "Wild Goose" chase. As the heavenly hand reached down one by one plucking up the weeds out of my garden, presenting each one to me as He dug down releasing the roots, I knew instinctively what it meant. He was promising restoration, pulling up the choking weeds that robbed the soil of its goodness, and preparing to plant something far better -- the crop He had been longing to sow for a long while as I had sought to defend my garden space. There I stood, no sword in my hand, only tears rolling in mighty streams down my cheeks. I had never felt such peace at the prospect of death.

A mighty warrior was my modus operandi, or at least that was my perception of myself, but it was all a ruse. Since the beginning of time it was the only way I knew to keep hurt at bay. The stronger my words, the harder my heart, the more distant my emotions, the more deadly the swing of my sword. I had left many unprepared soldiers in pieces on the battlefield, and in the moment of my humbling I saw the carnage, felt the pain, and wanted more than anything to make things right. *Why did I walk into every interaction like a war?* I needed to know.

Surrendering your armor, the chainmail and helmet hewn out of goods recycled from the past, is much like peeling back an onion--you don't realize how many inferior layers you have had to wear to maintain your peace and the removal of each one brings yet more tears. Tears that come from places you didn't know existed. Tears from many, many years before. Circles in the sand going round and round -- my repeating of patterns and God's continuous love for me.

CHAPTER 6

Sewing and Reaping

"They who sow in tears shall reap with joyful singing. He who goes back and forth weeping, carrying his bag of seed [for planting], Will indeed come again with a shout of joy, bringing his sheaves with him."

- PSALM 126:5-6 AMP

Patterns, like ones cut before them, will repeat themselves until we tire of the sameness of our outfit and seek a new fashion. If we expect the future to be any different than the past we need to pull out the pattern book and select a new style to wear. It isn't always easy to pick out something new, but having friends or loved ones in the process helps.

I was subjected to hours at the fabric store as a kid. I rarely remember buying clothes from the store. I became very adept at picking out complimentary fabrics, cutting out patterns, and walking on rogue pins in the family room carpet. There was nothing pleasant about sitting at those tables flipping through Simplicity and McCalls. I would pick out a dress I liked and my mother would point out that the style was not good for my body type and back to the books I would go to examine the sketches and figure out what made a dress look good or bad on me. I never did figure it out. At times it seemed like it would just be easier to make the same pattern as before with slight adjustments in fabric and size.

It always seems easier to go with what came before. The reduction of risk makes moving forward appear a little more conservative and safe. The problem with the status quo is that the outcome is constant and what you got the last time around will likely occur again not far down the road.

There were lots of circling back and spirals in my life. Relationally I couldn't connect, not in a real way, and when I did it was always tragic. I didn't understand the magnetic forces in my world, they were not like gravity that could be counted on, it was more like jumping off a bridge tethered by a bungee cord anticipating the kiss with the water below only to be launched upward into space -- unfulfilled. Or worse the bungee would snap, sending me plunging into the water below. A pattern had taken shape that was much like a neon sign pointing predators and perverts in my direction. I would get on the MAX train and be fully groped from behind. I would receive pornographic notes at work from a co-worker who was obsessed with me. I would date the "wrong guy"... the list was endless. It got to the point that I lived on hyper alert, always expecting a hand, an eye, a body, or a word to leap over the barriers of respect and steal from me the things I would not readily give away. Not knowing how to be free of the sneak attacks and invasions, I mostly hid, but sometimes I welcomed them.

Now hiding is the result of fear. Other than a friendly game of hide and seek, I have never known anyone to hide for any other reason but fear. Fear, when given power, will send us deeper and deeper into the woods. The problem with the forest is not the dangers from without, but the dangers from within -- the darkness that lies in our being that becomes one with the blackness of our surroundings. One can only remain hidden in such darkness in the absence of light. It is the place God is not.

As any botanist will tell you, it is extremely hard to grow anything other than fungus in darkness. So it should not surprise us that when we find ourselves dwelling in dark spaces, be it in our mind, body or spirit, the only things that will grow are molds, fungus, and infection.

Infections can be mild or life threatening. When we let an infection run its course, there is always a gamble: will it heal or will it kill me? I was pretty sure my infection would result in a long slow death, but it was the risk I was willing to take to keep secrets secret. My life documents were sealed and stamped clearly with the words "confidential" and "top secret".

It doesn't take a genius to figure out that stamping areas of your life as off limits is foolishness when you serve an all-knowing God. He will pull out those files and wait for *you* to present the materials, but He already knows what they contain. To think we can hide from God is a bit like a child covering their eyes and thinking they are invisible. It just isn't so.

From the age of ten on I held a secret that spawned many more secrets. The problem with secrets is that you can't have just one and when the secret is of your own violation and your subsequent discovery of sexual sensations... well, things get more confusing, more complicated, and hiding seems necessary. There is a deception, a covering, a hiding that cannot be done without deceit even if it is out of fear. Sowing deceit will bring a crop of lies, and a harvest of distrust.

Harvesting distrust was never my intention when I set out to plant my field. In fact, I was pretty sure I had grabbed the seed packet that would result in a "normal" life of wholeness. As I planted more and more seeds, I found more and more weeds. I was confused. I was trying as hard as I could to tend the soil and grow pretty things, but those dang weeds...

Weeds have a mind of their own, and the weeds of abuse and addiction, well, they stand to ruin everything if not pulled up. I think I was born addicted. The pattern took many forms over the course of my life, but the outfit looked much the same; a different color, a larger size, slight alterations, but the same current running underneath. Trauma.

The hidden currents in our lives threaten to take down the whole ship if we let it, and for me the undertow of my secrets and addiction was slowly pulling me, and everyone I let close, under. Certain things transpired in my childhood that made the transition from curiosity to full-on addiction easier than one would expect. Various addictions served as a great way of coping and avoiding what I was really feeling. As innocence was exchanged for questions, I set out to understand; to unravel the mystery and make sense of what was going on inside me, and yet to avoid just as much.

I was always a resourceful child. If I had a question, I would find the answer on my own. I was more private than most children and so my pursuit of information came mostly through covert exploration. At ten my sexual parts became known by the hands of another, at eleven I discovered myself, and at twelve I was regularly watching porn through the scrambles as I babysat late at night. Everything in me was convicted. I established rules and order and did everything I could in my pre-teen paranoia to make sure I was not found out. It was like a whole part of me was a separate sinful entity that was only allowed out under the right circumstances. Seeds planted deep, root deep, and will grow.

There are addictions and then there are *addictions*. If you are a woman certain addictions just don't exist, at least not in most people's minds, but there I was alone in my underground cave tending to my fungus. When life got stressful, I would tend my crop. As the crop grew, I would call a water shortage and the soil would appear barren once again, until the next time. Shame covered me as guilt whispered in my ear day in and day out, "*You will never be forgiven or loved.*"

Lies, when they come from within, seem more like truths than if they were spoken to you by someone else. I longed for someone to tell me I was loveable and worthy of forgiveness, but in the absence of truth the lies rang true and as time went on I became a master of the cover-up; of wearing just the right outfit to hide despicable me. I knew if you truly knew me, you would be appalled or disgusted, or worse yet you would rat me out and everyone would know my secrets.

It is funny to think that most of my life people have been drawn to me because I tend to not judge when you share even the craziest of personal stories. Maybe that is because I have lived a few myself, but more than that there is a deepness I desire from people. One of the greatest joys for me is to listen to people's lives and struggles. I have never known myself to not feel empathy and compassion for the pain and story of another. So it is ironic that I assumed the whole world would treat me differently than I would treat the world on the sole basis that I deemed my story and sins unforgivable.

As I understand it, there is but one unforgivable sin, if there are others they don't show up in my Bible. That sin is unbelief, and the result is eternal damnation (which still doesn't ring as the God of grace and love that I now know, but...). Since unbelief was not my sin, it was fully forgivable and a redeemable offense. It would take a lot of convincing for me to remove my cloak and reveal the chains that bound my ankles and kept me from running free, but the day *would* come.

The years of hiding were essentially decades of creating personas -- some knowingly and others manifesting on their own. There was the homely, lonely librarian. The emo chic. Eventually I settled with the persona I felt kept me most protected. I grew my bangs out, wore unflattering clothes (at one point opting to wear only men's clothes), buried myself in work, and pulled away from any and all social outlets. I had changed the look on the outside, but the inside still held the same worn out pattern and the minute I changed the outer appearance my old nemesis resurfaced.

When we sew the patterns of the past, we will reap the crop of history. Just like you cannot put new wine in old wineskins without them bursting. You cannot take an old tattered life and not expect to repeat the wars that shredded those garments in the first place. It is like laying a steak out in the forest and expecting it to be there in the morning. It is foolish to think that the predator will not find the prey and devour it as it has time and time again.

The circling within oneself, sewing the same patterns, is the unending quest to be found, but it will never be satisfied. Instead the repetition of abuse and addiction will drive us further into whatever protective devices we prefer. It isn't until we walk out to the mailbox and have a stranger read our mail back to us that we realize life doesn't have to be an endless cycle of victimhood and shame.

When those who have walked a path before us show up on our doorstep (the elusive "radiant ones") they will use words like "triggers" and "breathe". At first it feels patronizing and silly, and we wonder if these people understand that we are adults. It is all too much like a medical appointment as they ask questions to help you relax and get to the heart of you. As much as we feel parented in that moment and struggle against it, they know... we are trapped somewhere back in time. Just a child. A really lost and broken child.

As I had coffee with the women's ministry leader from church, days after my world had been tossed on its head, I sensed that my ship had not run aground just needing a good shove back into the current, rather it had been rendered dead in the water by what looked like from a distance, a harmless chuck of ice. It was no small thing, rather it was an iceberg whose surface was no indicator of what resided beneath. But she knew, and as she listened to me struggle against her suggestion, there was a look in her eye that said, "I am only saying this because I love you."

I instantly rejected her care and concern, but it floated like a specter in and out of my consciousness. God had sent a messenger, discerning things I never spoke aloud, and was not scared at my defensive walls and words. There had to be a way to close the door that I had opened by going to coffee, but like a rusty hinge it was bound, the sliver of light passing through the opening reminding me that it was, in fact, still open. As the days wore on the truth picked at me, pulling back the bandage, reminding me of the scars.

Scars, the permanent reminders of battles won and lost, revive at our acknowledgement of them, and like soldiers march before us in a great parade. I had my fair share of scars, some of them I wore proudly and others I struggled to cover up. If there had been a tattoo beautiful enough to detract from the ugliness I would have undergone the needle and let the ink do the hard work. But there was nothing I wanted permanently imprinted on me that might be looked upon as worse than the scar itself.

Scars and tattoos both hold a permanency that forces one to weigh the rugged beauty of the broken with the added beauty of art and expression. It was the expression that kept the ink away. I was not about to let you know what it was that gave me life and surged within my veins, just in case it was wrong, or bad, or disapproved. As much as I felt within, I had to remain neutral on the outside; a non-person with no wants or desires, likes or dislikes. I was a chameleon of every hue, changing to meet the shifting sands of my environment, to blend in and to not be noticed.

Living life as an enigma of sorts drags an emptiness behind it. You never truly exist, or in the least, people can't make heads or tails of you and keep walking. When you do make contact with the real world it is often surface at best. I had very few true connections growing up. I claimed my brother from the womb, but friends were harder to come by.

I had two friends growing up that I spent any amount of time with; Amanda and Stephanie. Amanda landed on our doorstep one day because her mom needed after school care (and would become a lifelong friend) and Stephanie, well, she was my defender.

Bullies come in all shapes and sizes. You can have everything going for you and out of the blue be subjected to the meanness of adolescence. I was fourteen as my sophomore year in high school commenced. As volleyball daily doubles began, I could feel their gazes, hear the whispers, and knew that I was in for it. I braced for the worst, trying hard to plan how I was going to navigate this next phase of life. The problem with raising yourself is that you have to raise yourself.

If puberty and all that goes with it aren't bad enough, learning to read the compass while you journey through can make it harrowing. As the girls began to tease me about hygiene and self-care, Stephanie stepped in. Now to have a strong force step in when you have survived on your own is a strange new territory. She didn't care about any of the external things, but I knew she would stand up for me. I surrendered to her protection and for a moment I felt like I could breathe.

It was breath that evaded me most when it came to social interactions. I didn't fit. I didn't know how to interact. I watched Stephanie and learned; learned to fight with words, to never let anyone know your weakness, and to show your strengths at all times. How to be tender and sweet, but guarded all the same. They were thoughts I was well acquainted with, but wonderfully new and empowering. And for the first time I was not alone in my battles. The pride that had told me for years that I was better than my peers, that I held a worth that no one could see, and that I was going to be something someday rose from the ashes with a fury of a firebird rising to flambé the enemy. With Stephanie at my side, I felt I had found not only a protector, but the best friend one could ever have.

Having a best friend, when you don't know what friendship is, is a little like swimming in a hurricane. The wind whips around your face, the water churns around your body, and there is an emotional rope that seems to keep you anchored. As the storm circles you just never know if that anchor will keep you from drifting out to sea or be what drowns you in the end.

Relationships, when you have never gone about them with proper guidance and direction, are confusing. I became deeply sentimental, as if the world depended on me maintaining the friendship. And though Stephanie never asked anything of me but to be me, I was compelled to figure out what it was that could tighten the bond, be it lusting after professional athletes or actors together, or just being interested in things she found interesting.

Bonding is an essential part of life. We come into this world and hopefully we bond with our parents, struggle to find our independent self, and then find equilibrium somewhere between self and others. Not having the foundation of a good bond and separation left me spinning like a tornado. Somewhere down the road there was bound to be a mess. I was finding out first hand the effects of lack.

Emotional detachment and lack of nurture makes for a sloppy mess at the table of friendship. There was always a hole, a deep cavernous pit in my stomach that pleaded for fullness, but no appetizer would suffice. You could serve up the best dish, yet all I wanted was to be held; to feel love in a tangible way. I would gladly surrender the food of flattery and the dessert of appreciation for ten minutes of your time.

The profound emptiness I lived with made no sense. I had a stay at home mother, a father who worked hard to bring home a decent living, and we always had food on the table and a roof over our heads. Everyone loved my family and desired to be "adopted". The confusion made me feel more and more defective as time went on. *How could everyone feel loved and cared for by my family, but me?* My mother must have been right, I was just spoiled... spoiled rotten.

Rotten fruit is a great attractor of flies. My rottenness, as I see it now, came from not tending to the crops more than an excess of sugars. Good fruit was left on the vine; abandoned, left to be eaten by the bugs and birds. It instilled in me the notion that I was not lovely enough to be picked, and I never would be truly worthy of love.

So when God started showing me His love I was more than overwhelmed, I was broken. It was like He was taking the overripe fruit that others saw as just waste and was gathering it to Himself. He had cider to make and the time was perfectly in season.

I love a good glass of cider, and an apple cider donut... well, I just gave away one of my weaknesses. The truth is the best cider comes with age and from apples that you wouldn't eat straight off the tree. The best cider apples are bitter due to their high acid level and other factors, but when processed, those same qualities that made the apple inedible add color, body, and dimension to the drink that makes it the marvelous creation that it is. And that is what God does, He takes our waste and the unpalatable parts of us and creates something tasty and good that not only He enjoys, but that others are nourished from as well.

I have come to believe that God is the greatest problem solver ever. We go about our lives, tear up our fields, let our produce go bad, and He adds in His love and grace and makes something wonderful out of all of it. I guess that is why I marvel everyday at His goodness. He never had to redeem any of it, yet He does -- over and over again and it is His pleasure to do so.

Redeeming broken places in our lives is what God does best. I think it is one of His greatest pleasures actually. The word redemption has taken on such intensity in this season of my life. I watch it unfold in so many ways and each leaves me a little more in awe of the power and love of God. It takes hold of my heart in such a deep way that I have a hard time holding back the tears. "Those who sow in tears shall reap in joy."

It is almost like a promise; the revealing of all of us and the surrender to His grace and mercy takes the fields we have planted, and with our tears of humility and remorse, washes away the topsoil ravaging what came before and then He prepares the soil for His seeds; the seeds of the fruit of the Spirit.

"But the fruit of the Spirit [the result of His presence within us] is love [unselfish concern for others], joy, [inner] peace, patience [not the ability to wait, but how we act while waiting], kindness, goodness, faithfulness, gentleness, self-control. Against such things there is no law."

~GALATIANS 5:22-23 AMP

So in Him, the endless cycle of my sowing bad things comes to an end and the beauty of Him can take root. On my own I would just cycle through my known patterns, planting more and more of the same, storing up barns and silos full of harvests that are worth nothing and will go to rot and become a dwelling place for rats and vermin. His amazing grace takes my offering of a poorly tended field, pulls up all that is not good, amends the soil with His goodness, and plants the seeds that I could not procure on our own. Insecurity told me I was a bad gardener, but pride had kept me from seeing that I was not a good farmer. God stood by waiting for me to ask for help. And when the moment of truth was revealed He wrapped me in His love and began to cultivate the soil of my heart.

CHAPTER 7

For the Love of God

"Deep calls to deep at the [thundering] sound of Your waterfalls; All Your breakers and Your waves have rolled over me. Yet the Lord will command His lovingkindness in the daytime, And in the night His song will be with me, A prayer to the God of my life."

~ PSALM 42:7-8 AMP

I sometimes wonder why people say the things they do like, "For God's sake...", usually followed up with something like, "...pick up your clothes." As if God requires our complete perfection in menial tasks. Or, "For the love of God, just do it!". It is like every parents' last ditch effort to force us into obedience by insinuating that we don't love God if we do not obey *them*. It sends so many mixed messages to us as we grow up. For me it reinforced the notion of a demanding God.

Overwriting the tapes that have played for decades is hard. You pull out the mixtapes, play them through, reminisce a bit, and wonder if you really want to sacrifice that tape to your new mix or just put it back in the box for later. That was how my experience with grace and love was... I had some new favorite songs, but my tapes were full of nostalgia from previous seasons. To hit record and overwrite what came before was a struggle between the heart and mind and the choir of voices singing along to their favorite tunes.

The mind has an uncanny ability to convince us that what we know to be true is, in fact, an untruth. The compiled data is sorted, and whatever pile is bigger is the "correct" answer, even though it may not be the most compelling data. It is much like reading case studies already gathered together with similar outcomes and deducing that this other study you came across cannot be correct; though the study group was larger and method of data collection more stringent. It isn't that it can't be correct, rather it goes outside your idea of what should be. God's love is like that.

As I struggled between my old ideas of God and this new loving God who was singing over me, I kept finding myself wanting to believe His love was true. And though my previous data suggested otherwise, the more I walked, the more I was convinced that God was much more than a gracious God who pardoned me of my sins on the cross. He was a jealous lover and a loving father.

My father did his best to love us when we were kids. I spent Saturdays in the garage and the yard alongside my dad and in a lot of ways those hours, his time, was what I thought of as love. The glasses of water at bedtime when I stalled, that too was love in my little mind. But to feel comforted, safe, and secure in able arms was something in Hallmark movies. So when God began to show me tangible love I was overwhelmed.

It was late February at this point and my best friend had come to town and a little gathering of church women had been scheduled to share in a time of worship and prayer. I made a surprise appearance (honestly, I wouldn't have missed it for anything!). But as my friend was leading us in worship I just felt a familiar depth come alive in me. A song shot its arrow into my heart and I broke in such an unexpected way. It was His love that overwhelmed me and my brokenness cried out. I hadn't noticed that the head of the women's ministry, the woman who had read my mail months earlier, had taken the seat next to me until her arm was around my shoulder. Where normally I would have pulled away and collected myself, I collapsed in the acceptance of my brokenness. There was a purity of love in that moment that eclipsed all fear. I cried as she held me, then I cried more as I sensed the motherly love of that embrace. When she said, "You are sooooo loved baby girl." I lost it completely. For the first time in my life I cried before others knowing that I was accepted and loved in such a real and tangible way. It wasn't her, though it was. It was God and I was His child whom He cared for deeply. And a new, deeper understanding of love broke through overriding what came before.

Understanding the care and love of a parent is something some people take for granted. For me, it had always been a hole that went unfilled, like a pothole that just grows bigger the more people drive over and through it. And when that pothole became a sinkhole, I began to swallow people up in my need. Had I understood that no person on earth could fill that hollowness, I may have stopped looking in all the wrong places and sought God sooner. Instead, when people failed me I turned to books to try to figure out what was wrong with me.

Have you ever noticed how bookstores always place the religion section right next to the self help books? It is like they are saying if this doesn't work try this, and if that doesn't work try this. And in a circle we float between wisdom and understanding, yet never really come to the heart of things. That was the story of my life -- seeking to understand all the wrong questions.

Too many hours of my days over the course of my life were spent trying to unravel what was wrong with me. *Why was I so defective? How I could change myself or my behavior to get the desired outcome?* Striving left me navel-gazing and unable to look up and see God's open arms. After reading half the library, filling my head with more information than a college degree and getting nowhere, the prospect of surrender seemed like the only real option. All my knowledge left me cold, but that embrace... that was the comfort I longed for.

Being okay to be a child when you are very much an adult is foreign and brings up a sense of neediness. It makes us lay down our pride and surrender whatever it is that we think we can control, and just sink into His arms trusting that everything we feared we would be rejected for is covered by His love. Accepting God as Father changed everything for me. I thought the love of God was good, but to lay my head on the chest of Father God... well, nothing is more calming than His heartbeat.

When you can hear that steady pulse of the heartbeat of God, there is the assurance that you will never be alone, that He will protect you no matter what, and that He is able to meet your every need. Prayers become conversations, and in that intimacy there is a connection that cannot be rivaled. It is breathtaking to take in a Father who is so perfect, like wave after wave crashing over me, flooding me with the knowledge that I am loved.

The ocean has always held a special place in my heart. My family visited the beach often and I would spend hours walking along the shoreline, watching the tide crash upon rocks and toss logs ashore. The day I was overtaken by a sneaker wave was traumatic, but it taught me a great lesson: never turn your back on the ocean. I remember at that moment being concerned not for my well-being, but for my brother whom I had coerced to hunt for shells with me. It is interesting to me that when God's love crashed over me, my focus instantly turned to those around me. It was like I could not not tell everyone about the love I had found.

There is a passion to share when you are moved so deeply, that to keep it to yourself seems selfish. I had spent years in my selfish stupor.

To go back to that place would be to spit into the eye of my Father who had given up everything He valued for me to live. For the first time I longed to serve Him not to earn His love, but to abide in His love and to grow closer, more intimate with Him. In His love my selfishness was apparent.

Few things scream for my attention more than the selfishness of my own ways. They really are like small children constantly underfoot. I think the reason God made our selfish tendencies so needy was so we would always have an opportunity to acknowledge them. Selfishness, or really anything pertaining to the protection of self, is a toxic poison to our system. It infiltrates every cell of our being, riddling us with cancer until we allow the radiation treatment of the Spirit to lay its full conviction upon us. It is easy to start stowing away things and forget that it is selfishness at its core that causes us to hoard the good things in life.

Growing up I had a problem with hoarding. It was like I couldn't fill my shoebox any fuller. I didn't want anyone to have my precious shells, rocks, pressed leaves and four leaf clovers. I would store away my treasures in fear that someone might take them or destroy them. In some ways I feel like that is what we do with God's love. Instead of sharing it, we hide it away in our hearts. We keep it to ourselves. The problem that arises is that some of us never get to experience the love of God, just the words. That was how it was when I was a kid. The love of God was a concept and words. No one ever told me how wonderful it really was or could be.

A lot of people don't get the chance to experience the real deal when it comes to God. They are told God is this religious entity and neglect to mention that the relationship can be, and is, real. It is like being told you are eating lamb, but really you are being served mutton. If you don't know the difference you can go your whole life thinking you don't like lamb. Mutton is tougher, fattier, not even close to the succulent, melt in your mouth, tenderness of lamb. It is gamey and takes some acclimation of the taste buds. But lamb, nothing is better than a perfectly prepared leg of lamb (oh the difference a year makes!). Mutton may have been a lamb once, but it was very much a sheep at the time of slaughter. To think, you could eat a thousand sheep and never once taste lamb... I guess it is very much like how we can read every verse about love and never truly experience His love. You can settle for mutton and call it lamb if you want, but it is the wholesome nourishment of lamb that I long to eat and serve others.

Jesus as the Lamb of God was hard to take in as a child. I understood the sacrifice, but I could not comprehend why it was a lamb. Sure, lambs were cute and it seems like a horrible sacrifice to make when you look into their cute little faces, but Jesus as a lamb made little sense. To understand the sacrifice you have to recognize that the lamb was spotless, at the peak of perfection in every way. It was a great sacrifice for any family at the time, and Jesus was the greatest sacrifice God could make of Himself for us. My little mind saw blood and sadness but missed the love of sacrifice somehow.

Sacrifice, as defined by my young mind, meant sharing. From my third birthday on, the word I heard most often (besides being called "bossy") was "share", and sharing was a daily requirement. Sharing meant giving up my things so someone else could enjoy them. Looking back it seems like a form of martyrdom, but really it ended up like environmentally influenced codependency. And what should have been a beautiful lesson in love turned into teeter totter with one seat on the ground while the other was stuck in the air. After a while neither child is having much fun.

So with my bad teeter totter experience lodged in my mind, sacrifice was not about giving something precious to another, it was simply death. Death of everything. Gory, bloody, and otherwise. There was a longing to understand what receiving a sacrifice would be like, but to have the opportunity seemed impossible. I was the giver. The world held the takers. I had to be okay to be like God and just keep giving to no avail. And so I lived my life, never believing that I was worthy to receive love.

When the mind decides that it cannot and will not ever be loved, the best solution is to kill the desire. The issue that arises with killing the desire to be loved is that God created us to be loved. It's foundational and necessary for us to live. I have often joked that I should be dead hundreds of times over based on the psychological principle of affection: "We need four hugs a day for survival. We need eight hugs a day for maintenance. We need twelve hugs a day for growth." Yup. I am dead thousands of times over! A hundred was a very conservative estimate.

Growing up in an environment that was more like a desert when it came to affection, versus a lush valley that some families offer, you learn survival skills. I swaddle. The day I was forced to admit this fact was when I realized how much anxiety I had when I was not wearing layers of clothes, or wrapped tightly as I slept at night. There was a security I could offer myself through the tight wrapping of layers, that though they appeased the body's request for touch and to be held, left no real comfort for my longing heart. Like so many other things, I took on a substitute and called it the real thing. Due in part to the guaranteed safety of self-pacifying, I killed off another foundational system of my being physical relationships.

Our physical bodies are created with eleven intertwining systems; there is the circulatory system, the digestive system, the endocrine system, the exocrine system, the lymphatic system, the muscular system, the nervous system, the renal system, the reproductive system, the respiratory system, and the skeletal system. None of these systems can function properly without the others. Our internal physical complexities are not so much different from other areas of our life. So it reasons that when you begin shutting down things like desires and longings, dreams and hope, you leave yourself to operate sub optimally as a life form God never created you to be. Add to that lies about ourselves, and what we are worthy or not worthy of, you have a child of God who has a faulty understanding of life and will continue to fail to operate successfully.

Successful execution has always been my goal. Hand me a softball bat and I am swinging for the fences. Basketball in hand I will sink every free throw. A thirty page report on Rembrandt and his use of light... you've got it (even after my computer dumped the file in the wee hours of the morning and I had to rewrite the entire paper from memory because I refused to outline on the front end)! To succeed was never a question until I found myself at my end staring out over a vast emptiness from the ledge of a cliff. There was no turning back, but to keep going forward looked like a certain failure. I had settled for so many things that never gave me what I sought, and to jump, well, it didn't seem so reckless. I didn't feel loved and protected or safe before no matter what I accomplished, and looking down at the lingering clouds below looked a lot more like a soft cushion than water molecules hanging in space.

To feel safe, one needs to know they are loved. When you don't have a reference for love, you settle for a facsimile. When you don't know the difference between knowledge and experience you can easily settle for what your mind can take hold of. I created a world that made sense to me, where I could design just the details I needed to meet specific requirements to ensure my survival, but none of it was to God's standards. He saw the fractured me and longed to reunite the pieces. He wanted so much more for me. So much less effort. More surrender to His perfect restorative presence.

The presence of God is often talked about in mystical terms which leads to a lot of discussion about how one goes about abiding in His presence, but it is pretty simple really. God is love, and if we abide in love we abide in God, and God abides in us continually. His Holy Spirit dwells in us and is our guide into all Truth. So it all comes back to love.

God's love is His very essence. To take hold of that truth is to find the greatest depth of understanding, but it is equally alarming if you do not know what love is. For me, to reach out for the uncertainty of love was a trembling hand half expecting to be slapped. But because He knows me so deeply (and always has), He came personally to me in a way I could not deny or resist. He compounded the message of His love through those radiant ones who had been brought through the fire; refined by His grace and mercy and love.

It was the intimacy of God *with* me that caused my heart to long to return the same depth, but to do so would require I relinquish my ownership of myself and allow Him to place *His* name on *my* story. It would mean opening every chapter, reading every word, confessing every lie, sin, and shameful thing. And like any story written by a master, it would not be destined to lie on a shelf collecting dust but to be read. Over. And over. And over again. The thought rattled my bones and shook me to my core. *Could I find it in me to be that vulnerable?*

Vulnerability, defined as "capable of being wounded or hurt as by a weapon", takes a great deal of courage. And when you believe that the God of the universe is asking you to walk into the truth of all you are, that can be a scary place. As I looked into the eyes of those around me and struggled with my own history, I knew the Lord was asking but one thing... to take His hand and trust in His love.

Taking my Father's hand as He escorted me down the dusty path, His voice smooth and confident, He reminded me of who I was and who He was to me:

"You are my child, whom I have chosen."

"You are worthy of My love."

"You are a new creation."

“You are sanctified.”

“You are born again.”

“It is I who draws you near.”

“My Spirit resides in you.”

“My grace is sufficient for you.”

“I have redeemed you.”

“I am your Savior.”

“I am your protector.”

“I love you.”

...I was loved. And I could not stop the tears.

CHAPTER 8

Mountains To Climb

"Who may ascend onto the mountain of the Lord? And who may stand in His holy place? He who has clean hands and a pure heart, Who has not lifted up his soul to what is false, Nor has sworn [oaths] deceitfully. He shall receive a blessing from the Lord, And righteousness from the God of his salvation."

~PSALM 24:3-5 AMP

It had been almost a year since that fateful day crossing the bridge and life could not have been more different. There was an uncertainty, a stirring deep down, an anticipation of greater things to come. For the first time I could see healing in the distance and it shone as brilliant as a diamond refracting the sun. Had you explained that surrendering to the process was a complete abandon of self I may well have run the other way in a state of panic, but as I stared at the mountain before me it beckoned to me.

I love uphill climbs. If I could only hike uphill and never have to come down I would be the happiest hiker on the trail. So when I began the trek toward the mountain of healing there was an excitement that boiled within; percolating with visions of what I might see and experience as I reached the summit. I was not prepared for what was ahead, but I knew God knew... or at least I hoped.

Having faith in a God whom you had just decided has your best interest in mind is like picking up your favorite book and reading it again for the first time. Each page you turn you know that you should know what comes next, but every time you are pleasantly surprised by what follows. It is hard to explain what it is like to live in the Christian world most of your life, leading people in their spiritual pursuit, and then out of the blue the Truth hits you. People look at you sideways when you relay your conversion experience from days before. You can't deny that you have lived two lives in many ways (maybe three or four or five), but the reality is, saying and doing the right things does not a righteous person make. It isn't that you never knew what you believed or even what the Bible said, but in an instant something resonated on another level and there is an understanding, a move of the Spirit within you, and the recognition of God as a loving Father who wants only the best for you -- His child.

As the mountain trail loomed, there was a new security knowing my Father was leading me and that I would not be alone. There was something peaceful about looking up at Him and taking His hand. It was like walking on air really. Like I was the belle of the ball. I felt incredibly special and cared for.

I hate talking about God in emotional terms or in pictures that might take it a step too far, but sometimes my prudent measures take away from the actual experience. What I will tell you is that I had never felt so loved, so cared for, so protected, so cherished in my entire life up until that point. The instant changes in me at that moment left me shaking my head as well. I held a compassion and care for others that I had not had before. I was forgiving of others. I held different attitudes and a greater level of acceptance both of myself and others. And because it was like being in a foreign country I had a whole new language to learn, new customs to understand, and a whole new outlook on life, but somehow it all seemed easy, organic... like being born again.

Being born again is a unique adventure. It isn't raising your hand at an altar call. I did that when I was twelve and though I felt good about myself it was mostly just ceremony (as was the chilly baptism in the Pacific Ocean). It isn't a prayer. I did that a hundred desperate times and even in college, and though it touched me deeply and God met me there it still did not have a deep lasting effect. I knew God existed and I could actually pray to Him, but my heart remained the same. But the moment I was laid out, broken before my Lord and His love filled me, that was different. It was like little pieces of me had been sacrificed over the years. It was a reboot. It was like you had you, then I "accept Christ" at camp and you get "You 1.1". Every repentance prayer adds another number or decimal place, but you are still the same person, just a slight variant here and there. But being born again, it isn't even like a 2.0, it is a completely new name. Don't ask me what that name is... but it is fabulous. It's fresh. It's new. It reflects the beauty of a new creation; not done by my good works or even my "want", but by His Sovereign hand only.

It was the goodness of God that took time to get used to. I was used to games. Of having to figure out how to solve the puzzles to get the right answer to get the reward, often expecting one thing but getting quite another. When the rug got pulled out from under me I always thought that was the test. Sometimes it was, but this time it was like God was pulling me close and reminding me there were no tricks, just a hard climb and His strong, confident hand to hold.

God is not a God of bait and switch, in fact, He often doesn't do anything He has not told us ahead of time. The misunderstanding comes when we neglect to take it all in, when our easily excitable minds eagerly grab for words we want to hear and ignore the rest. And that is how it was as I strapped on my boots and prepared for the next leg of the journey -- a bit naive, but ready to conquer the world.

When one sets out to conquer the world it is best to have an army and a plan. I had neither an army (I had three people I knew would have my back), nor a plan. To execute this technical climb was going to take skill; skill I did not have, and a knowledge that the wealth of self-help books I had read could never seem to afford me. With all reluctance, for it meant more vulnerability and nakedness before my fellow man, so I sought out a Sherpa to navigate the harsh terrain. As I dialed the number of a local trauma counselor, humility had run its full course, or at least that was what I had concluded.

In the culture of mountain climbing it goes without saying that you hire a guide. The Sherpa knows the mountain like the back of his or her hand. Both the Sherpa and many who have come before you have walked this ancient soil soaked with blood and tears. And yes, it is true, some never make it off the mountain, their bodies left in the ice and snow steps away from the pinnacle they sought (even with the most skilled guide).

One never knows when the journey begins if they will reach the summit. Maybe it is the moment we leave the basecamp that solidifies our decision, but to start out on such an epic journey one has to believe that they can and will see the top. It is insane really, to strap on a pack, risk complete exposure to the elements, sleep on a mountainside night after night not knowing if a blizzard will overtake you. There is a trust that comes from nowhere, that goes beyond your ability, and in that humility of taking the hand of God and your human guide you discover what you alone could never have found -- the best route to the summit.

Most mountains have many paths to the summit. Given the season or conditions, the ability of the climber, or various other factors the guide decides where best to place our feet and set us on course. To say that the guide is all knowing is false (that is why we need God on the journey as well), they too are at the mercy of every decision good and bad we make along the way. If we get fearful, if we begin to not use our oxygen correctly to support our ascent, if we push too hard too fast, or misstep and dangle over a crevasse all those things will force new decisions to be made which can alter the course -- sometimes for the better and other times for the worse. I was determined not to misstep, but equally determined to summit.

To slow a sprinter mid-stride is a little like throwing a spike strip before a speeding car. There is always the chance that it will end in a crash. I have always been, what my friends call, intense. I prefer doggedly determined, but the unvarnished truth is that once I set my mind to something no one better get in my way. It is all "go big or go home". And that was how I stepped into the river of healing at the base of the mountain of God.

The river ran swift and cold, but it invigorated every cell of my being. I had never felt so alive, so present, so able to cognate and understand. I couldn't do enough or run fast enough. The chilly waters had awoken the heart of me, rejuvenating me in a way that brought out the child in me.

At forty one it is a little odd to find yourself talking and acting like a child, but that was exactly what happened. As I walked into my kitchen, a teddy bear that had been given to me as a Christmas gift had become lodged in the crook of my arm. That was all it took. I had unknowingly picked up a stuffy and pulled the trigger on the gun of memoriam.

Strange things happened along the forest creek as I headed up the mountain. I would find myself talking in the voice of my five year old self to people who were not there saying things like, "You are mean to me. You can't be my friend anymore. You have to leave. You hurt me." Frankly, I thought I was going out of my mind. It would take every ounce of mental fortitude to pull me back from the brink. Something was being unleashed from within and I feared I was no match to keep it down, hold it back, or retain any semblance of sanity. *Who was this child? Why were they here now? What was happening?* (I know now that this had been happening my whole life without my awareness.)

The peculiar nature of the mind is that it can protect us one minute by shutting down and at a later time jettison information for us to process. It is like the ship can't maintain balance and something has to go. The personality has to split to keep calm in the midst of the storm. As my cargo had begun to shift in the swells of the sea, my mind sought to lighten the load. Years of flipping switches to avoid the problem were about to express their gratitude, much to my discomfort.

Switching gears and shutting down were prevalent throughout my story. If I was spoken down to and made to feel small, I shut down. If a sexual scene showed up in a movie or TV show, I shut down, even to the point of falling asleep. If someone physically drew too close to me the feelings would overwhelm me and again, I shut down or in my zombie state acted out. And emotionally I lived shut down for decades. So when I found myself at a worship practice staring at a keyboard and not being able to tell you what it was I was looking at, it frightened me, but it wasn't out of the ordinary. What was exceptional was the intensity of emotion flooding through me.

Being emotionally present intensifies things. For years I had not had a single anxiety attack. I accredited it to my amazing strength of emotional maturity. Anyone with half and understanding of life will tell you that to not feel is to not be human. It isn't maturity on any level. It is surviving, half dead and barely breathing. There is no life to be anxious about.

I had spent a lifetime surviving. What made my survival unique was that my trials and struggles were not seen by most. The things I protected myself from were internal and hidden like most everything else. Had I come from an alcoholic home or been beat on the roadside, it may have actually been easier to grow and mature because the journey of pain was out in the open. When everything remains hidden you die a slow and painful (if you allow yourself to feel it) death.

The dilemma one finds them self when an injury is easily concealed is that you may actually need medical attention, but you can opt for self-triage. Self-triage is complicated and rarely renders the desired result. It is nearly impossible to apply pressure at the proper angle, the diagnosis is usually inaccurate, and the wounds never heal or if they do they are a willy-nilly mess of stitch scars that end up being the dreaded conversation starter. If you are lucky enough to escape without scars there is always the hemorrhaging of the soul to contend with and the memories of the battles.

Trauma, the internal bleeding that few rarely address until it is too late, is an injury that is not quickly diagnosed and tends to affect the whole of the body and mind. We feel the pressure, the strange force that drives us to more pain, but fail to recognize the throbbing deep down is a sign of blood pooling as we slowly bleed out on the inside. It is our own secret struggle that drowns us from within and drains all life and hope from us. What makes our condition more dire is when we don't remember what it was that caused the injury in the first place.

There were blank spaces in the story of my life, that for years I foolishly believed didn't matter. The weight filled my pack, but I would look inside and not see anything, but it slowed me. I could feel it. It was just invisible, somehow hidden from view but affecting me all the same. Some say that the hidden things are best left unseen and that to dig around in hopes of finding something good, well, that just won't happen so it is best to leave well enough alone. Well enough was what had taken me to the desert and I was done with sand, now eying the snow just beyond the timberline. It would be a climb, but it would be worth it. If only my pack didn't seem so heavy.

The heaviness tugged at my shoulders; my chest crushed with anxiety. I could not go another day carrying this load. It was a burden. Waking to the second anxiety attack in twelve hours, I didn't care what it took. This was not going to happen again. I turned to my guide and we set out on a new path up the mountain, but this one held more ice and a cool breeze whipped past my face taunting me as it nipped at my nose.

It was colder than I expected the day that I broke through that layer of ice to reveal a face I had not seen since childhood. Frozen, that menacing grin staring back at me, I could not deny his presence nor the flood that began to surge forth in my mind. It was like the floodgates opened and the memories crashed over me, pelting and submerging me in a torrent of recollections of the horrors of that day.

I sat in my car, as alone as ever, the scene flashing through my mind, my body shaking like a leaf in a storm. I wanted it to stop, but I knew that to turn off the movie and walk away would only leave me to freeze in this place on the mountain. My pack was getting heavy, shortening my steps everyday. I sobbed tears the likes I had never known as my body convulsed, my heart pounded out of my chest, and my stomach longed to empty its contents.

To feel sick when there is no physical ailment is an indication of a sickness of the soul. The heaving came from the depth of a hole so far below that it felt as if my stomach was rising up to meet me. I was purging the contents of my subconscious and reliving the pain held so deep within. As the visions came to a close, the curtains shuddering the scene once more, there was peace in the terror. To say it was otherworldly makes it sound mystical, but it was very real, more real than any memory before or since. Clarity and revelation poured forth like a waterfall on the steep slope. Things that had been question marks, seemingly unattached to anything, finally had a home. The horrific madness of it all held purpose beyond anything I could have known.

Being abused, no matter how big or small the offense, has a way of stealing from you things you never realized you had, like innocence and the feelings of safety and trust. In the aftermath there is a change in the air, you see life dramatically different than before. For me, every touch held a nuance of something else, every conversation was suspect. Had I known what slept in the blank cave etched into page 3,645 I may have not felt so awkward and confused growing up. It was like I had built my whole life around a mystery and that looming question mark threatened to take down the whole structure. The dominoes had begun to shift and one by one they would reveal something greater as the momentum ran its course. There was a cleansing of heart, mind, and soul taking place as each cavern was slowly emptying its contents along the steep mountain trail.

CHAPTER 9

Snowballs and Cannonballs

"The Lord is my light and my salvation-- Whom shall I fear? The Lord is the refuge and fortress of my life-- Whom shall I dread? When the wicked came against me to eat up my flesh, My adversaries and my enemies, they stumbled and fell. Though an army encamp against me, My heart will not fear; Though war arise against me, Even in this I am confident."

~PSALM 27:1-3 AMP

Turning loose your will and allowing healing is a bit like chasing snowballs down a long steep slope. The further they roll the larger they get and the harder it is to keep up. I am a good sprinter and though I am built to run (probably forever), I never had the attention span to run any distance. Sprinting gave me a reward far faster than running cross country, so I never trained or anticipated needing marathon-like endurance.

Endurance and perseverance, though I often ignore them, are very much a part of my nature. I actually look forward to a fourteen mile day on the trail. And that was the irony: I always believed the faster the better, one and done, get on with things was the way to go, and yet I would gladly saunter along for a day out hiking giving it no thought at all. The truth is, when things are hard we want to get past it as fast as possible. When it is peaceful we want to dawdle and take it in a bit more, take some pictures, explore a spur trail. But the difficult stuff; the gut wrenching, soul twisting moments; well I would rather run my fastest and hope not to face plant, than to tread cautiously on the loose soil. After all, there is only one way to outrun a bear -- go fast!

The writer of Hebrews tells us that we are to run the race, but he never quite tells us what the race looks like. He tells us to strip off all the unnecessary weight, remove our sins that stand to trip us up, and to persevere, but fails to reveal the true nature of the course and competition leaving us with the reminder of what our Lord suffered. I don't know about you, but I read a lot of suggestion in there. I think it is fair to say that it will be hard, take time, and challenge us in ways we won't be able to endure if we are carrying a lot of baggage. We are to be aggressive in our pursuit, but nowhere does it say our "running" will be fast or without suffering.

Suffering is not something I do well. I will do just about anything to avoid suffering. Suffering is the opposite of joy. In fact the dictionary says the antonyms of suffering are happiness, health, and joy. I avoided suffering at all costs, but the three things to expect on the other side, well, I had no idea what those were.

Deciding to turn off the faucet of emotions as a child leaves many words without definitions. I had no idea what made me happy because I didn't know what "happy" meant. Health meant I wasn't sick, though I often found myself stricken with bronchitis and other ailments. And who could forget the chicken pox that ruined Christmas? And joy, well, joy was a word that rang out in songs but to identify it emotionally was beyond me. So, in my lack I suffered, though I thought I had escaped the grasp of suffering. By having no needs and only caring for the needs of others I robbed from myself happiness, health, and joy and suffered in the silence of my poverty.

Poverty, be it physical or just of the soul, is abject. To say that it is anything less than miserable, hopeless, and humiliating is to deny the reality of what it is. It was the poverty I tried to hide, the lack that I could not let people see, the emptiness that I did not know how to remedy. I stuffed the emptiness with achievements, with activity, addictions, and with the perceived needs of others.

The need to be needed is a devious character. It masks itself as lovely and helpful, but in the end leaves us bound and others wounded in ways that seemed unavoidable. The vast majority of my life was seeking to fill that need. It was all in goodwill that I sought to help those whom I saw as weaker or in need, but underlying it all was a brokenness in me that would leave me high up in my tower when the relationship changed, and others in the dungeon below struggling to regain their freedom.

To be taken captive unknowingly is a fearful thing. To not feel or understand what you are inflicting upon another tends to cause more injury than one thinks. Looking back I see the error of my instinct and the lives rendered crippled and limping, some to this day still lingering in their own brokenness. It is much like dragging one out to the wilderness and beating them silly and then wondering why they aren't following you home at the end of the day with a smile on their face. They are prisoners of war; a war they never enlisted in, and a battle they were not prepared to wage, captive under the guise of love, suffering under my reign.

The concept of suffering and the reality of suffering can be considerably different, and one rarely sees their affliction of others. I was oblivious. Suffering did not really exist in my world as far as I was concerned. I was in constant need, but it didn't seem like suffering. Suffering happened out in the world, in other people's lives, in history.

History has held a great deal of suffering and it was the measuring stick that I held against my minor discomfort. I had a pretty good idea as I walked off of the bus and onto the grounds at Dachau what kind of suffering went on during WWII. I was not prepared for my dormant heart to awaken from slumber, for the numbers and faces to penetrate my soul, for the anger to rise up within me as I engaged with a history where innocent people suffered (for no good reason), and died out of obedience at the hands of evil. I had negated the effects of suffering in my life, believed it did not exist, but the suffering of others was real and I wanted to stop it. All of it. I could not see my own actions or life reflecting back at me, though the images pierced me deeply.

Where once I sought to mother and comfort and shelter, I now saw myself as an advocate -- the one who would speak up on behalf of everyone else. My rescuing became chronic, and like an addict needing their next fix, I couldn't help myself as I walked into relationship after relationship with people who wore the scars of AWOL parents and vacant homes and all sorts of abuse. I was the fixer, the lover, the one who would make everything right. What I could not see was the need I was longing to fill within myself as I slowly suffocated my victims or fell into their cleverly laid traps.

When you set out to rescue someone or attempt to fill a void in their life, it is a fallacy; an apparition of the mind, to think that you can actually pour enough of yourself in to satiate the need of their soul. And when you don't have authentic love, the probability of your portion even making a dent in the need is next to nothing. I gave and I gave and I gave. There was nothing I would not give if I thought it would bring life to someone. The more of myself I poured in, the less I could see of myself, the more empty everyone became.

To fill a vessel with water you must have a supply and a means of replenishing your source. I walked the road of life with a broken vessel that at times had but a few drops of water in it. I would pour as much spiritual understanding as I could into my jug, pray for the continuance of blessing and that the reservoir would remain full, only to find at the end of the day I had lost all I worked so hard for. Through the cracks and fissures all the goodness seeped out, and my emptiness was made more certain by my giving to others. Day in and day out I sought to fill me; through reading the Bible, praying, leading study groups, and prayer and worship times; but time and time again the jug remained empty.

When you take hold of the Truth and find the God of grace you realize that striving and being perfect are not a means to get anything in His Kingdom. Becoming a servant to the King, He takes your broken vessel, carefully fills the cracks, and then He fills it. You don't have to put a quarter in the machine. You don't have to select the flavor. It is a simple act of presenting your vessel.

I have always had an issue with worthiness and pride. I am pretty sure I am right and you are wrong, but I am ashamed underneath it all. If you want to challenge me, well, I will probably not back down without a fight. When the Lord began to break my heart, He did ever so gently by calling out my pride and reminding me of my worth.

The problem with pride is that it demands to be right, longs to be known for all the wrong reasons, and tends to seek its way. When God stooped low and I realized just how low He had to bend to reach me, there was no room for pride, the encounter itself was humiliating in all the right ways.

The thing about God that I can't understand is how He knows just how to undo me with no force, no coercion, no commanding of my submission. It is like I melt in His presence. I can't fight against His goodness any more than I can live a successful life apart from Him. Even in my most rebellious moments He would call back my heart from the brink and I knew He would be there if I was willing to lay down my sin and pride, but I was so unwilling.

The Lord is a gentleman and He waits more patiently than He ought for us to come to the end of ourselves. As we pile up our snowballs and ready for the fight of our lives, He waits. As the snowballs roll down from the summit, He looks on and wonders how hard we will run after them, and what it will take for us to surrender. He empathizes with our situation, but He waits for us to come to our end.

In any situation there is the opportunity for passivity or activity. One sits back and waits for things to happen, the other is what forces the first to get off their butt and get moving. I was always the latter, the change agent, the visionary and one to give the swift kick to the behind. When the time came for me to receive the kick, I jumped a mile high, stunned that I had become so complacent that a prodding was necessary. I quickened my pace and ran through the snow hoping to rise to my full potential.

It was on the mountainside as the snowballs began to cascade from the ridge above and the ground began to shift underfoot that I knew an avalanche was about to change the landscape and held the force to ruin me if I fought against it. All my past weaponry fell from my pack and a swell of white enveloped me, encasing me in the cold snow.

As the rumbling came to an end, my body locked in a cocoon of snow and ice, there was stunned silence. I had survived. I was alive. I wasn't free, but I could see light through the layers of white. I drew up one hand and began to claw, shaving away the snow around my face, and on the other side were voices. They were digging down. I was digging up. I was certain no matter how hard the journey was from here on out, the worse had already overtaken me and I was alive to tell the tale. I had surrendered to the elements my weapons, and my life was intact and God had seen me through.

It is when you breach the surface that you see what it is that buried you; the layers of sin and pain and everything else you sought to outrun over the years. And it becomes evident that those little snowballs; those tiny fibs, the indiscretions, had all rolled down the hill to where you lay. It is in the warmth of the sun that you sense a moment of relief, for the Son is removing the sins of the past as you surrender each one to His piercing rays. They begin to melt away...

To surrender our snowballs is relatively easy. The sins like gossip, envy, even theft and lying, they all are just little things that we created on a whim and then as they carried on down the mountain became a larger problem, but we look at them and understand that God can melt them; dissolve them in the warmth of His love and forgiveness. They were mostly innocent, self-protective infractions that got out of hand, but nothing God can't redeem. But as the snow melts away under the summer sun we find the remains of a war, the cannonballs of the larger sins spawned from our pain, that have sat and now request our attention.

Coming to the end of yourself, surrendering your snowballs, feels freeing until you remember that a war has been raging for years under the surface. As the winter passes away and the casualties of war come to light, we are forced to reckon with the weapons of our warfare and the sins of torment. We trip and fall over the cannonballs of our past. We come to a moment of decision: admit the wars exist or fight the reality.

Decisions should come with warning labels, like "DANGER" and "May cause the following side effects...". It would only seem right, and give us fair warning of what we are getting ourselves into before we make the leap, but it isn't that way. We never quite know the big picture until we dive head first into our choice. The choice is not to fight or to run, but rather to allow yourself to be overtaken or to be crushed under the mighty weight of it. Sin will always take you down, but the hand of God holds forgiveness if we allow ourselves to be washed over by His blood. The more you attempt to push back against the inevitable weight of conviction, the more broken you become. It is not His strength that destroys us, rather that we break bone after bone as we try to hammer our way through this life without Him, or somehow think we can do better than Him. And that, in the end, is the greatest war -- not the war that we wage with the world, but within ourselves and with God.

It is folly to believe that we can save ourselves or dig ourselves out of the pit. The only way we stand to go is down, not up, as we chip away at the walls of our personal hell hole. The only way to rise from the depths is to come into the light, and that requires our humility, and the decision that we will take hold of the hand reaching down into the pit of our sinfulness and be willing to expose every disgusting bit in the light of His love -- not just our snowballs, but our cannonballs as well.

Cannonballs, carefully formed and loaded into cannons, ignited and hurled onto the battlefield of life, well, they are far more destructive than our measly little snowballs. And as they roll downhill or bounce across the field, it is very much the scene from "The Patriot"; heads are taken off, blood spurts in every direction, every friend or foe in the wrong place at the wrong time loses. It is when we have to face the cannonballs that we will struggle with the most guilt, the most shame, and attempt to pretend they don't exist. But they do, and as we pick them up and try to gather them and hide them away, we understand the full-weight, the lead, the anchor that threatens to sink our soul.

There are sins and then there are *sins*, and the moment a sin can no longer be hidden, is a moment of complete horror and yet unexpected relief. For me I was good at confessing my shortcomings, even my failings (though it was a sucker punch to my ego), but to come clean and bring out into the open things I could easily keep to myself... well, I was convinced that God would never forgive me. There was guilt in the snowballs, but confessing my sexual sins felt like shame and it was bound to a whole lineage of shame.

When the founding elements of one's life are tainted with abuse, shame abounds. I am uncertain if I remember a time when the voice of shame was not echoing through my mind. It was much like another family member that was always at my side. And though the beginnings of shame were not my fault, and the subsequent steps I walked out were very much dictated by what came before, shame continuously told me I was damned.

Shame is a villain of the most dastardly sort. It is our internal nemesis that has nothing better to do than to remind us how defective, inadequate, unworthy, disgusting, and unredeemable we are; though none of those things are *actually* true. Covered in shame we isolate ourselves and create rifts through all our self-protective measures of anger, jealousy, and anything that can cover our flaws. These cannonballs of sin must not ever be seen!

Cannonballs are made to fit in specific cannons, and unlike snowballs, their size does not change over time, but their destructiveness can be monumental and reloaded time and time again. They come to rest after their momentum has done its damage, just a token of the war and a reminder of the carnage. In our shame, we see the blood residue and we believe that those things, those cannonballs and all their destruction, are somehow beyond God to redeem.

The thing about cannonballs is that they are made out of lead. Lead, though disastrous on the battlefield and seemingly as hard as a rock, melts at 621 degrees. To put that in perspective, you can melt lead on your stove at home in a cast iron pan. And that is exactly what God sees when He looks onto our collection of lead rounds. He sees the sin for what it is, and longs for us to surrender them like all the others. And in the moment that we come to our senses, ignore the shouts of shame, and perceive that we have believed a lie, God takes those cannonballs and begins to melt them down (not unlike the snowballs). He places the dirtiest of sins that we have sought with all our might to conceal, into His smelting pot and melts them down. Not only that, He takes the melted lead and pours it into a mold, creating a beautiful reminder of His redeeming love and the forgiveness of even the most shameful of sins. It is the testament we carry from that day forward. It is a sign of His mercy and grace and the reminder of what came before, not so we are shamed by it, but so we can be thankful and rejoice in His overwhelming love for us.

As I approached the cannonballs of my life, I found sins; sins I didn't want to see, some I ignored completely hoping they would just go away. But lead is heavy, and even if you don't acknowledge it, it will weigh you down. I had found such deliverance and healing in the months since my first encounters with a loving God. I almost had forgotten all that came before, but in the back of the closet I had tucked away the worst of the worst, hoping God wouldn't ask me to bring them out for show. *Maybe He could just absolve them without me having to truly confess them…*

Confession holds a unique place in the Christian walk. Though there is no mandate to confess our sins to anyone but God, it is wise to confess our sins to one another. I am an extremely private person and the thought of sacrificing my pride with my peers to relieve my conscience was, and is, terrifying. But as I journeyed further into my healing, it became apparent that to bring my confession before another was necessary, if for no other reason, accountability going forward. So, trembling in fear and insecurity and wearing my shame, I expressed all the darkness of my past sins and addictions and of the present struggles that threatened to undermine all future relationships.

There is a clarity and unyielding peace in surrender. It was not easy. It was somewhat embarrassing. But it was not at all what I feared it to be. Surrounded by the relentless love that consumes all doubt and releases all shame I felt the weight lift. The cannonballs were surrendered and a beautiful sculpture was placed in my hands as a memento; a statue to be looked upon as a reminder that the past was indeed in the past. The cannonballs, like the snowballs have been reformed by the Creator Himself for His good pleasure -- to show the world His redemption and love.

When the Lord does redemptive work, it is easy to think in myopic terms. We see how wonderful it is for us and disregard the heart of God within our sphere of influence. Our world is not ours. We may function in a certain way and within the confines of a group or environment, but God created us to be one with all of His children. We are family. We are all one in Him because in Him we have a common Spirit. When God sees His child holding out a willing heart in all humility and He does His great healing work of redemption, it is for each and every one of His children in that moment, not just the one who is going through the process. His heart is intensely corporate in His individual pursuit of us.

We were created for community, and community requires vulnerability. We embark on the quest knowing each of us holds our own strengths and weaknesses. We rejoice when others rejoice and weep when our comrades weep. Our testimony, His testimony alive in us, is our strength and encouragement. It nourishes us as we journey on, reminding us that we are all in this together, and in that there is peace.

For me my first foray into community was a bit of a shockwave to my system. I quivered in fear at the prospect of being known, every hair standing on end as I walked into the intimacy of strangers. I felt the need to expose my true self. And though I fully expected to be rejected like so many times before, what I found was acceptance. It was curious. I didn't trust it fully, but there was a sincerity; a seriousness in their eyes as I spoke and they listened. It was like these people really cared. And I began to think that people might actually hold the ability to love me.

CHAPTER 10

Iron Sharpens Iron

"As iron sharpens iron, So one man sharpens [and influences] another [through discussion]."

~PROVERBS 27:17 AMP

I have always been a bit of a loner. Give me a good book and I will retire to a comfortable place along the river and just read. Sometimes it takes a real effort for me to not be a recluse. So when God kept pressing the issue of community and relationships, I squirmed like a kid who had sat too long without a recess. The marbles in my pocket were crying out for my attention, but God had other plans and He wanted my full undivided attention.

When God has your best interest in mind, in my experience, there is a great deal of stretching that goes on. The discipline of stretching is something that neither I nor most of my clients over the years have been any good at. We do it when we hurt, but seldom do we undertake stretching as a regular exercise or as a precautionary measure (my husband may be the one exception). So when God starts elongating the muscles of character it brings discomfort and we fear that pain is not far off, especially because life is not one, but a series of partner stretches.

Thinking of life in the context of stretching muscles puts a whole different spin on things. When people test our patience we are forced to recognize how tense we have become. What we find is a stretching session we weren't anticipating. When we have to share our story for the first time it is scary, but the more we do it the easier it becomes. We stretch the muscle. And like with vulnerability and love, it is the active stretching of those muscles that allows us to grow and become who God made us to be -- a part of a community.

Whether we like it or not, God created us to dwell with and among one another. None of us was born to live alone on a mountaintop, though we may have seasons where we feel very much alone. Or like myself, I spent a great deal of time dreaming of vanishing into the wilderness and living happily ever after. His heart from the beginning was for us to live and grow in community. The word community made me squirm. I had an aversion to community.

It was not anthrophobia, not even agoraphobia, it was athazagoraphobia. The fear of being forgotten, ignored, or abandoned. As much promise as a community of like-minded people held for true relationship and love, the ghosts of seasons past bellowed their moans of pain and cries of torture. It was hard to shake the feeling that I was walking into a trap that would leave me abandoned, forgotten and ignored in a foreign land having to fend for myself once again.

Feeling abandoned and ignored is one of the most desolate places emotionally. I hated it, but it was a staple of my young life and it followed me into adulthood. To survive I found that the sure way to avoid the crushing blow of abandonment was to need no one. If I eliminated the risk of relationship, then the outcome would be assured. Problem was, though I could not abandon myself. I also could not pacify the desire of the soul to be in community. The pulling and tugging at my heart the closer I got to God, well, it was not something I could avoid. On my own, my walk with God was good, but He knew that to go deeper with Him I needed my dullness to be sharpened through true fellowship with other believers.

They say the strength of the forge determines the quality of the iron, but truly it is the iron that sharpens iron. The forge establishes the iron, but it is the application of another (also created by the forge) that brings the sharpness. This is why relationships are necessary, not just with our Creator, but with people. A relationship with perfection is easy, almost predictable, but humans; they are a wily sort.

People dealing with people can be as ridiculous as watching a cat circus; climbing, hissing, jumping over one another, never the same trick twice. One voice starts an angry entrance to a conversation and what should have been an amiable discussion becomes an altercation. And that is why it is much easier to be alone. We know why we feel as we do and shouting at ourselves does little good, so why do it? We may have internal struggles between different parts of ourselves, of conscience and conviction, but things are relatively peaceful if we eliminate others. There is chatter, but it is familiar. I was fine to keep my world small--just me and God. We're good.

God, unlike people, doesn't get worked up when I shout. That is very nice of Him actually. When I get real with God, He doesn't back away or tell me to get a life or that I am stupid. He leans in. He gets a little closer. The relationship is not weakened, it actually becomes stronger (even if my words get colorful and are more reminiscent of a sailor than a disciple). I am not advocating we scream at God all the time, but being true to our heart and frustrations, well, He rather enjoys seeing us in our naked state versus the many strange outfits we often wear. The funny thing is, the way He accepts us and our humanness is what He desires of each of us as we take on each other in each of our fallen flawed states.

I will say, when I was invited to join a small group at church I was apprehensive. I was in the thick of finding my way on this healing journey and though I knew I needed supportive people around me, I didn't like the prospect of sitting in a room full of church leadership. I knew that my story would surface. I knew there would be questions. I knew honesty and integrity were paramount as I signed the confidentiality agreement, but I gathered my stones and began to construct a wall anyway. Maybe not a fortress like before, but at least a barrier I could hide behind if need be.

As week one rolled out, like a good student, I did my daily "homework". The topic "Who Is God" was so elementary that I rolled my eyes a few times, but as I stepped into the pages I was finding truth that I had not seen before. God had become so real over the previous six months, but to be grounded not in the emotion of who I knew God to be but in what the scriptures actually revealed Him to be was enlightening on a different level. I was awakened to an even deeper place of understanding.

Awakening from inaccurate understanding is a trip. So when the Lord asked me to hand over the rubber band ball I tossed about from hand to hand, I thought He was kidding. I mean, each rubber band had been carefully placed, it was years of study; of spiritual quest. I opened my hand and He started removing the rubber bands from the ball I had formed through religion and obedience. It was like He was making a gun with His finger and shooting the lies off into the distance, scattering them in the wind. And as He did He began to show me truth, not truth that I could juggle and put on a good performance with, but the truth of Him. His person. The attributes of God and not just the actions.

I don't remember ever not knowing that God existed. When I was a child some kids had imaginary friends, I had God. He was real, maybe just because if I allowed myself to think He wasn't that would mean I was truly alone. But no matter, I always felt like God was living and active. I wasn't sure what that meant other than I would be punished for my every wrong-doing, but I believed it nonetheless. Nightly prayers were rote and ritualistic, but I somehow knew that God was listening. I expanded the prayer a little more as time went on. "Now I lay me down to sleep. I pray the Lord my soul to keep. If I should die before I wake, I pray the Lord my soul to take. God bless mommy and daddy, my brother and me (yes, i prayed for myself...lol), grandmas and grandpas, aunts and uncles, cousins, little friends..." and every pet that ever lived. It was not a spiritual experience, it was an exercise to appease God at the end of a long day.

Laying the stones of acceptance and approval based on ritual and performance were part and parcel of my life. God demanded it. My parents expected my excellence. My peers looked to me as the steady and reliable one. In some ways the pressure to perform made me more skilled as life went on, and I was very blessed to accomplish just about everything I set my sights on. The conundrum one finds them self in when success is the only option, is that you walk through life only accepting the challenges that you know you will be victorious. I would only do what I knew I could do, or study and practice for hours before I would set out to "try" something in the public sphere. The result, people were amazed, I was heralded as a "natural", and I found at least some of the approval I so desperately sought (though I never heard the words from those who it would mean the most).

As I flipped through the pages of the workbook it became apparent that my fears of being rejected would be realized the minute the group reconvened. So when I found myself in the small group, sitting around the living room of my pastor's house, that all too familiar lump began to form in my throat. One by one people began to share what revelation they had received from the week's assignments and then I found myself opening my mouth.

I am not sure why I spoke up, the words just stammered out, not gracefully either. The fear of speaking the truth that I was rediscovering who God was just felt shameful, like why am I just now getting this stuff. Then there was the fact that I (the one known to have all the right words) couldn't speak a coherent sentence.

The words, like the staggering steps of a drunk just kicked out of the bar, wandered around the room. I longed to protect myself, but the words kept confessing my weaknesses, my spiritual deficiency that I had hid behind religiosity all these years. And I knew that this group would be the death of me. Not because I was not accepted, as was my fear, but because the word vulnerability began to ring in my head day and night.

Week after week I found myself not only relaying the truth about this new walk with God and the pieces of my history that had written the wrong messages on my heart, but I also discovered that no one in that room was judging me. That was the moment things got real. I was not ready to share the deepest parts of me, but somehow I knew that in that room I was safe and that God had safe places in this world where His children truly meant no harm... even pastors and leaders.

To feel safe is a strange sensation that most take for granted. I remember the first time I felt "safe". It had come only six months before as I spent the first night in my big empty house. As I laid there on my mattress on the floor, it was a feeling that I had no words for, but I knew deep down I felt safe. Safe like I was within the security of a mighty fortress. It was a feeling I was starved for and a feeling I never wanted to lose. At that moment I made a decision to disallow anyone to enter my fortress just as I had my heart.

Keeping people at arm's length (or farther) was the only response I had to maintain safety, but for some strange reason as I engaged in this group, the more I allowed the others in, the safer it felt. It boggled my mind. I began to journal and write about vulnerability, trying to unwind the reality coming to life before me. I could not deny that humility, vulnerability, and true community were bound in love and all would be necessary to weave the great tapestry that God had foreordained. There was a thrill and a horror at the prospect of being known that began to send me into emotional convulsions. One minute I was ready to connect, the next I would decide to quit the group. One day I was high on the new revelations I was taking in, and the next I was afraid that I would have to share my story.

Sharing our story should be a wonderful experience complete with grace, forgiveness, love, and redemption. My story felt like shame. Like I had been so daft and defective that somehow I missed the boat year after year. *How could one live the Christian life in a very public way and forty years later just be finding the Truth?* I had never been stupid, but I felt very stupid in that moment. And when I was asked to share my testimony it was like everyone leaned in wanting to know more. I backed out and instead shared a song I wrote almost two decades before that was very historically true to my life story, but it was a "safe" share with very little risk eloquently masked in imagery only I would know the true meaning of.

A little later everyone in the study had to share a three minute testimony within a group of three, and though I knew two of the women in the group were absolutely safe to share with, I felt awkward, ashamed, and more uncomfortable than I had been in a long while.

When the wheels came off and the brake shoes scraped metal to pavement, I feared the worst. *What if I bared my soul and I got beat for it? What if I allowed myself that one instance of vulnerability and that left me open for attack? What if I had already let these people roam around too long within my story and they were just waiting for the right moment to use it against me?*

I survived the three minutes, but just barely and the remainder of the night was a deep shade of shame. I remember driving home scared. Paranoid really. There was no way that I could ever be okay with being known. I was too bad, too ugly, too messed up for too long. God may be able to forgive me. But people? I was pretty sure they would be turning on me very, very soon. After all, humans could only be loving and accepting for a short while before they got tired of it. It only took a glimpse at history to prove that out.

The weeks that followed broke me in a way I never saw coming. As my personal journey of healing was commencing on a parallel track, small group was becoming a pleasure, and I started to actually look forward to talking and sharing with the dozen others in the room. I was feeling the pressure of metal upon metal, and I was becoming sharper and so were they as my story unfolded before them encouraging them in ways neither of us could have imagined. I was beginning to see and understand the mandate for community, for vulnerability, for love.

I do not want to make everything sound like all unicorns and rainbows, because certainly there were times I was broken beyond belief over the course of those weeks, and even as the thirteen weeks came to a close I was still very much protective of myself and my story. But that last night I was desperate to hold onto anything or anyone I could. Beyond my better judgment, I gave a handful of people "my story" (a document I had typed up as an exercise for myself to try to remember the key instances that lead to where I was now standing). What I had not anticipated was the hole that would be felt as I drove home from the final official meeting. It was much like that scared feeling weeks earlier only alongside the fear of exposure was the fear of abandonment. Just as the anxiety threatened to take hold, my ever-so-common state of ambivalence swooped in and numbed me.

In retrospect, I think a part of me was embracing the spontaneity of my vulnerability but an equal part felt like walking away from everyone and everything. That familiar feeling of being the lost child, left outside shivering and cold, abandoned. I was convinced that people only cared while in the group because it was what they were supposed to do. And history swirled like debris in the path of a twister, and I was sure I had been duped yet again. *How could I have been so stupid?*

My mother disallowed throwing boomerangs in the backyard. She was insistent that we take it to the park. I am not sure if she was untrusting of the throw or the return, but in theory it should always return from whence it came. For whatever reason, I too was always shocked when it did. Life, like a boomerang, has a way of whipping back around and flinging itself at us until it gets our full attention. No matter how fast I ran I could not outrun it. No matter how deep I hid, it found me out. The interesting thing about healing is that it only comes in our weakness.

Weakness is counter to my nature. I would rather you know how I overcame my weaknesses than to share with you the litany of my failures. But when you set out on the path to healing on the mountain of God there comes a time when the climb is too difficult, your strength is overcome, and your weaknesses are barred out on the slope of regret. You feel helpless and exposed. It is there, in the starkness of our weakness, where God's strength is perfected.

As I walked into church the week following that final meeting I was shocked to find that everyone was still there, and not only that, they had actually read "my story". They were not turned off by my imperfections and failings, but glowing with love and acceptance and longing to embrace me. I was thanked for my courage. Encouraged to be strong and to press forth, and approved despite my vulnerability and the truth that I was just now starting out on my spiritual journey. I was okay. They were okay with me. I still held a few secrets, but I just kept shaking my head at their acceptance of me.

I have done a lot of shaking my head on this journey. I must look like a bobble head most of the time, and I probably need to go to the chiropractor. None of what I have experienced could have been predicted and that makes for a funny story when you realize that I have always been the one to control my world. The new reality was: this was not my world and I was not God. Go figure.

It wasn't that I thought I was God, but somewhere in the pages of history, buried in the script of life, a note had been written that demanded I work toward perfection. I had taken that scrap of paper, carefully folded it, and had been carrying it with me for decades. The more I began to embrace vulnerability, the more I was challenged to accept my humanity, and the more I had to come to grips with the absoluteness of my fallibility.

I was taking in the journey, collecting trinkets and journaling my adventure, when it became evident -- I was not in control and I was not perfect, nor would I ever be. I recoiled. The truth of imperfection took a pin and stabbed it into my inflated visions of who I was and could be. As my balloon sank limply to the floor I knew God was sending a message, redirecting my focus, and instilling a new truth of who I was, and more importantly, who He was and who I was to Him.

The God I knew growing up and the God I was coming to know were completely different people. The love and compassion that my new God and Father held was intriguing and new every morning. I looked forward to every sunrise. Each day I felt His challenge to open myself up more to Him and to those around me. I wanted more than anything to be seen and to be known and accepted, but I still held that old fear that rejection was just a shout away.

To shake the notion that rejection is always lurking is like trying to get pine pitch out of your hair. It sticks better than some glues and when it comes right down to it, you will most likely just have to soak it in oil and comb it out. And that is what God began to do to my life. He began to apply His oil to my mind seeking to heal the deepest parts of my thinking and in doing so, my heart changed. I began to see and understand my humanness, my position and place in His kingdom. No longer did I feel compelled to live to prove myself; to try to be perfect. He was showing me the truth of my imperfection. Imperfection that He loved and embraced and cherished. I didn't embrace it as He did, but I was becoming more and more convinced.

Imperfection to a lifelong perfectionist seems idiotic at first sight, but as the words resonate and conviction grabs hold of the lies, there is that deeper knowing that stops you. You hang your head and tears begin to fall. It isn't that you have failed to measure up, but that you have failed to recognize your own humanity and the grief that overwhelms in that moment is the knowing that you have made your own "self" an idol. You have chosen to bow at the altar of self and praise the works of your own hands and laud your own achievements. The intensity of that awareness sets the world on a slightly different axis as God gently continues His humbling of the human heart. Being cognizant of the truth, well, it comes with a greater responsibility.

Responsibility is easy when we limit it to paying bills and showing up, but to walk in the truths that the Lord reveals, that is far greater indeed. So when I found myself carrying the truth of my imperfection, that I would never be able to attain a state of perfection, I resolved to be completely real, completely alive, even if it meant being a complete and utter failure. I was removing the safety nets I had so carefully placed in my life, determined to be as authentic and true to who I was no matter the cost.

The cost of complete authenticity is a high price. Rejection is a multimillion dollar industry. So when God kept hammering the nail of vulnerability and tying it to the word community, I absolutely knew where the road was leading. What I found as I handed my weaknesses over to others was compassion on a greater level than I had ever seen. Even more, as I shared vulnerably with others they began to open their hearts and souls to me as well. It was like a garden slowly coming into season. One bloom. Then two flowers. Then three, and four... What was once just a plot of dirt and weeds, had been given a few bulbs in the ground, and now those bulbs had shoots rising up and flowers revealing their beauty for all to see. For the first time in my life, I truly cared more about others than my own self protection. I was getting mushy. The tender heart within began to beat with a passion to love no matter the cost.

Choosing to walk wholeheartedly into love is amazing in ways I never expected, but it does require that nothing is hidden, nothing is withheld, that no matter the possible risk you have to be willing to be real. Being real obligates us to be known, and being known means scars and all. And being okay to be "average" and imperfect meant transparency on a whole new level. It meant turning on the projector and allowing God to lay my life on the screen to be projected on the wall; no edits, no overlays, just the truth that I was not as perfect as I would like to portray.

I have pursued perfection for as long as I can remember. With the absence of praise in the areas in which I strived, I never felt good enough, strong enough, or just enough in general. That ache longed for relief so I set out on a crusade to find the hidden gem of perfection.

Perfection, when we finally figure it out, laughs at us in a mocking sort of way. In the moment we recognize that perfection is reserved solely for God, we must resolve to live in imperfection. Imperfection, as we know, means we have weaknesses. My world was crumbling before my eyes, but as it did, it revealed a treasure more brilliant than the perfection I sought. It was the beauty of humanity.

For the first time I began to see people as stories to be read and experienced. Each was a mystical place of adventure. No two were alike and yet we were all very much the same. We all were born sinners, all held strengths and just as many weaknesses. We were all very much human with wants and needs and desires. We all had unmet expectations, dealt with heartache and grief, and struggled with God (if we dared to admit it). And that was the door that opened before me offering to me true community and love. I did not have to perform. I just needed to be. I was to be present in body, mind, and spirit and engage with my fellow humans. There was no expectation, but to bring my iron and apply it to the iron of others. My well had been empty for so long, but the water table was rising...

CHAPTER 11

Water In The Well

"O God, You are my God; with deepest longing I will seek You; My soul [my life, my very self] thirsts for You, my flesh longs and sighs for You, In a dry and weary land where there is no water."

~PSALM 63:1 AMP

To drink the Water of Life, to take in the pure refreshment of who He is, requires an emptying of yourself. As long as our cup is filled with our wants, our needs, our stuff, there is no room for God in our vessel. I had spent so much time over the years attempting, ill-fatedly, to fill myself up and to satisfy the longings of my soul that I did not realize I was staring into a deep dark empty well.

A picture came to mind the other day as I reflected on the process of my healing. I sat down at my computer to try to render an image of what was vivid in my mind. As I did, I found myself pulling and dropping pieces and moving things about almost like an animation. When I concluded the image was a mess, but I had witnessed, in real time, exactly what God was trying to show me. We all have holes, some deeper than others that we spend a lifetime trying to fill.

The image began of a child in the desert staring longingly into the deepest pit. It was a rather rugged hole, but reflective of a well in the ground. The desert was dry and foreboding. It was like the only life that existed there was this child. As the child leaned over the ledge and stared down into the emptiness, a tear fell, and then another. One by one the tears gathered at the bottom of the well, each droplet its own little treasure falling into the darkness and emptiness below. The tears went on and on and on. And soon rain began to fall. The rain, just like the tears, streamed down into the hole, and I realized these were not rain drops, they too were tears -- God's tears. And as I looked into the hole I could see the water rising and in it words like "courageous", "loveable", and "beautiful" swirled about in a waltz of words in the glistening blue water. It pierced me to my core. I knew the hole was being filled. By grieving the loss of what came before, through the surrender of myself to the process of healing, and the truth of who I was and who God longed for me to understand who He made me to be, the emptiness was being filled. The words were truths meant to remind and sustain me, my water in the empty well.

Words are my friends, always have been and probably will always be, but there are some words that are for the rest of the world and not me. As the child's tears fell and transformed into shapes and then letters, the result was too much to bear. It was not that the words were not true of me, they very much were, but I had never allowed myself to think those things of myself. Though I was very prideful most of my life it was actually insecurity. I had always seen affirmations as phony or applicable to someone else, but not me.

I have always seen the best in people and the potential that others may overlook. I also held a special measure of compassion for the less fortunate. In some ways all my outward attention made me feel better about myself, yet none of it made me feel more accepting *of* myself. I saw myself as strong, but never strong enough. I was smart, but could always be smarter. I was never enough of whatever I sought to be or do. So when God began to speak His words of affirmation over me, I struggled to accept the words. As He held me close and continued to whisper the truth of who I was, my heartbeat slowed and little by little I relaxed into His arms.

Reason when given full reign will override every heartbeat that longs to speak in constant rhythms to us. The peace that rested on me as I allowed those words to be heard was refreshing as a summer's rain. And as I rested I knew my heart was syncing up with His.

Unless the heart is injured in some way it is the best time keeper around. It speeds up when we speed up and slows down when we slow down. It is like God made us to be in sync with our hearts, not the other way around. And when we fall into step with the beat of our heart, we simultaneously fall into rhythm with Him. Then begins the dance.

To find our true heart and walk in step with its steady beat, we have to be honest about every longing and desire. It was unnerving to me at first. The idea that God was asking for all of me -- every last bit -- seemed like a lot. That every moment of my life *had* been for *His* glory. That even in my most despicable moments He was there. That the desires I was unsure were okay, were in fact, placed within me by Him. It was from the beginning His plan, His purpose, His pleasure. He longed for me so much that He sought me and indwelt me.

There is a magnificent place where God and myself come together. I mean, we have been together all along, but when it is truly realized... You see when God created me He joined two lives, His and mine. Maybe that is why my story is *His*tory. The joining of the Creator with His creation. The indelible mark of God on all that I am and have ever been and forevermore will be.

Creation is a miraculous and beautiful process of becoming. It can also be ugly and messy and terrifying. My life reflected the both/and of creation. I knew firsthand the feeling of creation. I had art and things I made with my hands, but in my story my greatest regret led to a creation all its own. The creation of a life. Induced by a moment of unrestrained and unrequited passion that would terrorize me for years to come, I found myself trembling as the panic set in. I was pregnant. There was no way I could allow him to know. I had to distance myself from him. I had to find a solution to the problem. I had to fix things and set the world right again. It wasn't rational, nor was it in alignment with any thoughts that had come before. But as fear flooded over me, I had to eliminate the creation I never asked to create. The resulting termination of the pregnancy would ever be under the surface. That was my most hidden secret that I knew would never go without judgment. It was my deepest, darkest secret as far as I was concerned.

As a creator I knew the power of creation, but I also lived out the horror of my stewardship of *His* creation. The shame of destroying the beauty of His design forced me to compartmentalize yet another part of me, as I continued down the path of less certainty and more internal torment.

History goes forward as much as it goes backward. It is reflexive in the sense that all of what has been makes us all of who we are, and all of who we are is creating all of who we will be as He redeems the parts to make us whole. He made no mistake when He created us and His restoration is to the exact specifications of His *original* design. He knew what I was going to do before I did it and stood by as I rejected His help. There is no amount of shattering that has occurred that He can't reform into a whole again, no broken thing He cannot and will not redeem, no life that He will forget or neglect. He will fill our well with living water... if we let Him.

I lived my life so thirsty. I just shake my head. He truly has always loved and cared for me, even when I was far off. To be chosen from the foundations of the earth. To know He formed me just as He so desired. It strikes to the core of me. *How could I ever have doubted or not believed in the possibility?*

Unbelief, be it of God or anything else, is a dark hole that longs to be filled. It is a place of self-sufficiency and lack. A land where one is never truly satisfied and there is always more striving to do. It is the spot that says, "This is the life!" until it isn't and we find ourselves empty once again looking for the next rollercoaster to take us back up to a new height of understanding.

I always loved roller coasters. Something about the rises and falls and the way your stomach launches into your throat only to drop down and compress your bladder seconds later, the turns that jerk you in such a way that you are sure the car will leave the tracks and you will plummet to the fairgrounds below. There is a thrill safely contained (we hope) within the limits of the ride. There wasn't a ride or roller coaster I wouldn't want to try as a kid. But when the roller coaster of life refused to stop and the conductor just waved as we passed the gate once again, I found faith harder and harder to come by. The highs and lows helped me to know I was alive, but the sadistic nature of the conductor felt menacing and threatening. *What was God waiting for? For me to be thrown from the car or for me to slip under the bar and jump out of my own insanity?*

I wasn't thrown from the car, but as my car entered the intersection I was broadsided and spun into oncoming traffic. I was eighteen at the time, struggling with God, my own guilt, and an eating disorder. It had been eight days since I had acquired my license and probably just as long since my last full meal. My little blue Volkswagen was my prize as I drove home from a scorching hot day working a sidewalk sale. I am wholeheartedly convinced that I had a green light that day as I was hit in my passenger side, the seat collapsing over the center console and coming to rest on the edge of my driver seat. As the car spun and glass sprayed around me I heard a voice, "I have you. You will be alright." And as the car came to rest in the front end of an oncoming vehicle in the middle of the intersection, and I had not a scratch on me, I knew. God was protecting me. *Why?* I couldn't quite understand.

When God extends Himself into your world, when you have all but turned from Him, you have to take notice. The comfort in the moment I heard those words was unlike anything I had experienced before and, until recently, since. It made no sense to me that God would care for someone like me. I was choosing a path of slow death, defying His rule, and making my own way in life. I was confused by His presence.

And not having a belief that God could speak to us, I kept my experience to myself. I knew it was real, but I had no way to prove it.

The supernatural, be it good or evil, had moments of occupation in my life. A number of times I witnessed strange things that nature and science could not explain, and at times I was more fearful of evil than I had been of God. When the darkness seemed to be creeping in more and more I believed that this was the result of playing Ouija Board with my grandmother as a child, as if everything I had been overcome by was the result of my sin, and I deserved everything I received. Given the fact that my faith was all but gone, I asked Satan to show himself in an unmistakable way and if he did, I agreed that I would follow him. As the night sky split in two along a diagonal (it very well could have been an illusion of my mind) I knew I was playing with fire and feared I had lost all hope of heaven. Interestingly enough, I had asked a similar question of God when I was little, with much the same result.

My life and my theology were barely shadows of the truth by the time I was midway through college. And though I was attending Bible classes daily and inundated with commentaries and lectures on God, I still did not know what it was I believed. *If God was love, then why did He allow such terrible things to occur in my life? If God was merciful, why did I feel constantly guilty and shameful? If God was everything the Bible said, why could I not see and understand it?*

In the back of my mind I held a lot of questions about God, but I had learned early and often that you don't question God. You learn and accept what is taught about Him. If you have an honest question you are to go to the concordance and study until there is understanding or seek out a leader or teacher to discriminate between truth and error. In all my self-sufficiency I never asked the questions out loud. In my study I filled my head with copious amounts of knowledge all the while my heart withered and faded within me. It was a pattern I danced in and through time and time again, never quite understanding the dance or what it was really for, because at the end of the day I knew a few more facts, but I still felt empty.

Trying to fill the spiritual hole within me has gone through many seasons. There was the fall of despair that made me question everything. The winter of walking away. The spring of coming to the end of me and planting again in the ways of righteousness. And the glorious summer of basking in Him. But when I look back there were very few summers, or even weeks of summer that I can remember. Flipping back through old journals I am struck by my longing to have more of whatever it was God had to offer, but time and time again the words ring of striving and religion. My heart aches at the words written by my own hand. Had someone told me that more study was not the answer back then, maybe I would have come to this place of greater understanding before this year.

The paths in life we take are often not straight and narrow, they twist and turn and leave us in precarious situations. We strive and work to no end to prove our life is complete and that God is fine being just a crutch and a spirit somewhere that we throw a desperate prayer to on occasion. I am certain now, every minute of our wandering breaks His heart.

I ate the bread of idleness while feasting on my busyness of working myself to the bone even to the point of complete exhaustion. He knew I was thirsty and starving, but I thought the emptiness in my stomach was just the result of my past, and the only way to get through the day would be to ignore it and hope that it went away.

When you are starving your body goes through stages. There is the moment you realize you are hungry. You deny it for the sake of comfort. The bodily reminders of your emptiness -- the longings that require you to silence their screams for your own sanity. Then there is the outright revolt of the body, where systems begin to shut down to maintain survival. To starve in a desolate place of lack makes sense, but to choose starvation when the Giver of all good things stands before you with the Bread of Life? Well, it reveals the stubbornness of one's heart, be it motivated by pride or shame.

When you finally reach that last thread of self and reach down, grab the scissors and take in that final deep breath, your heart skips a beat. There is a trepidation in your movement, but the ache deep down cries so intensely you cannot ignore its moans. You realize that this last act of courage could send you plummeting into the depths of who knows what below, but to continue to hang, to dangle before the certain death of denial, well, that would be a much slower more painful death. So with one desperate prayer for your life to be spared, you reach for your knife and cut the line. As the last fiber grinds across the blade you close your eyes and apply the necessary pressure. It will all be over soon.

To fall into the arms of a loving God in complete surrender is unlike anything I have ever undergone. I had every choice in the world to not obey, and yet I felt as if I had no choice at all. Humility spoke to my heart in such a way that I could no longer deny what my life had been, my story demanded I own it, and I knew God had written my name next to His on every bit of it. To be brave in that moment meant to give up; to hand over the history (all of it), to surrender the pain, to release myself from the suffering and shame that I put myself through for so many years. To be free I would have to die... completely.

Dying, when one has undergone a resurrection, feels at first like you are the fool of someone else's foul joke. There is the thought that something in all of this is just not right, and yet, it appears that is exactly where life has delivered you. The appearance, as deceptive as it is, elevates the depth of all the fears you have carried your whole life and makes you question everything. *Is this really worth it? Does God really require this of me?* When the questions beg for clarity, God smiles.

The human in me struggles to understand the humanness of God. It seems almost irreverent, but deep down I can sense it. He knows everything I feel and can empathize with my every thought, desire, longing and regret. He knows what it is like to look death in the face, to come to the end of one's humanity and cry out to divinity. Every struggle. Every tear. He knows them all, has felt them all, and has captured them all.

To think of God capturing our tears in bottles, as we read in the Psalms, astounds me. *Why would you cherish such symbols of hurt and pain and distress? Is it not enough to live it once?* To hold onto them and the memories seems like a depressing epitaph etched into a tombstone. But I am called to remember that all tears are not filled with sadness. There are also tears of joy, of celebration, of laughter that also get collected. It is the wholeness of our emotions that reflect the heart of us. It is the jar filled with our story that He holds so carefully in His loving hands. We are precious to Him. *All* of what makes us who we are, every little bit of us, and every step of our journey.

In the desert the hole fills with the tears of truth and the story of life overflows and pours forth. We are no longer who we once were, but we are also not who we are becoming. It is a great transformation that only the Master knows what the result will be. To move into what He has for us we must look at the puzzle pieces displayed on the table and watch as His hand gently takes ours and assembles each one into the image of His design.

CHAPTER 12

The Puzzle of Personhood

"I will give thanks and praise to You, for I am fearfully and wonderfully made; Wonderful are Your works, And my soul knows it very well. My frame was not hidden from You, When I was being formed in secret, And intricately and skillfully formed [as if embroidered with many colors] in the depths of the earth. Your eyes have seen my unformed substance; And in Your book were all written The days that were appointed for me, When as yet there was not one of them [even taking shape]. How precious also are Your thoughts to me, O God! How vast is the sum of them!"

~PSALM 139:14-17 AMP

Life is such a jumbled mess of pieces sometimes. There are times I look at all the different shapes, sizes, and colors and can't make heads or tails of any of it, and yet everyday I press in, curious as to what the interlocking pieces will reveal. The more of the picture I see, the more excited I get.

I have always loved puzzles, any kind of puzzles really, but nothing beats a really difficult jigsaw puzzle. An interesting thing about me and puzzles is that I like to solve them as fast as possible, and without looking at the box as a reference. I sort all my edges out, gauge (from memory) how the image will be scaled on the table before me, lock the edges in place, then I begin the tedious, but necessary, step of sorting all the remaining pieces by depth of color, or distinct design or features. And then it is like magic. I will look down and pick up piece after piece and before long, the picture begins to take shape. The more of the picture there is, the faster the pieces fall into place. Just thinking about it makes me want to go buy a puzzle. But I don't have to, I am living it.

As I set out on this journey I had no idea what was missing from my life. I knew I was broken. I knew I was dissatisfied with life and with God. I thought I knew what I was doing and how to live my life, but as God began to open my eyes to the reality of what my life had become, it was obvious that my table was full of pieces -- some of which weren't even to my puzzle and others were missing completely, or had fallen to the floor in one of my fits of rage.

I had taken many pieces over the years and tried to force them together. I had an idea in my mind what I was supposed to look like and I smashed the tabs and blanks together as I saw fit, not realizing that the image was not at all what God had in mind. It wasn't completely wrong, but there were shades that weren't quite right, lines that were incomplete, and there was always a fear to venture from the edges where aesthetics hung out and move to the middle where the true person of me resided. *What if I didn't like her?* It was a very real fear.

Growing up I was uncertain about everything about me. I had no references to base my understanding on and so I observed. I watched others. I gathered data and began to build the great Frankenstein I would later become. I knew who I didn't want to be, that was easy. I didn't want to be the girl who people picked on. I wanted to look like I knew what I was doing. I wanted people to like me. I wanted to be good at everything. I wanted to portray strength and not weakness, control and not submission. I watched the Bionic Woman and empathized with the struggle of being human and superhuman. I wanted to be her, to be able to save humanity and meet the Six Million Dollar Man and maybe make a go of it. Oh, Lee Majors... Anyway, there was a toughness that I needed for survival, and I had to discover a way to compress the emotions that drove me to deep empathy and sympathy. So I gathered the pieces and started assembling the puzzle that was me.

When you begin picking out the components that will in the end be made into a masterpiece, you typically have some ideas of what you are looking for when you peruse the shelves of the craft store, or at least some people do. I am a creative at my core, but where my strengths reside are not where most begin. I like the tedious. I enjoy creating something out of less than optimal circumstances and materials or completely out of my imagination. I always found the craft store a bit overwhelming, and it felt a bit like cheating. My mother on the other hand is a lifetime member of Crafters Anonymous.

My mother is a crafter. There was always a glue gun warming somewhere or fake flowers waiting to be arranged. Her skills were so good that she made a living taking artist clay and forming it into characters and objects, even to the point of funding my college education. I trusted her skills, but not her judgments when it came to the creative process because, as I saw it, we were one hundred and eighty degrees away in our likes and dislikes. So when my mother spoke into my life things like, "Why can't you just do things like the other kids?", "Why do you have to be so weird?", and "If you've got it, flaunt it." I was unmistakably uncomfortable with her suggestion, and I soon rebelled against any and all advice in regard to my life and my appearance.

I will readily admit, my idea of style was not that of my peers. I would try to be trendy, but somewhere along the lines I would miss the mark. I remember in Junior High the trend was spandex leggings and an oversized t-shirt pulled to the side and through a decorative ring. My mother's friend had me pick out the material of my "custom" leggings. I was excited and loved them. I had no idea that for most of Junior High everyone was just laughing at my design choices. As far as I was concerned they were excellent and perfect -- a true expression of me.

Expressions of me are hard to find when you flip through the pages of my life. The few glimpses you do see are quickly squashed under waves of harsh criticism or misunderstanding. As a result, I found fewer and fewer reasons to express the me I knew would, in the end, be rejected. *What was it about me that made me always feel like I was on the outside looking in?* The question plagued me in the worst way through some of the hardest seasons of my life. People always *seemed* to like me, but no one ever truly felt there. Then again, nobody ever knew the real me.

So when God began moving in my life in a new and outrageous way, when it came time to reclaim the person of me, the familiar fear levitated up to eye level reminding me that this could turn out to be a complete disaster. But this season was different, I knew it deep down. I took the hand of God on my right and swung with my left to clear the path and knock down the mocking specter of my past. It was an act of faith and bravery, birthed through determination, and acted out through my new dependence on God. I began to pray like never before. *Please God show me who it is You want me to be…*

God's ideal for us is pretty simple. He wants us to be the sum total of our longings and desires that He placed in us. Walking into the healing path, I had no idea what those were. The terms alone, at first, made my skin crawl. As Christians we weren't supposed to have wants and definitely not desires. Many years swimming in churches and ministries had made that clear. But the more I read, the more I understood. The more that God spoke to my heart, the harder it was to deny His heart and the reality that He made me to desire true love and intimacy.

There is a physical softness you feel when your heart begins to melt after the cold long winter. As I pursued my identity, I found myself with greater questions than "Who am I?" and "What am I supposed to do with my life?" I discovered that those things are very much the outgrowth of the inquiry and not the questions themselves. The only question God was asking was, "Are you Mine?" And if so, the outpouring is assured -- love. I thought I was getting into a list of things I would change or reorder to accommodate a "new me" on the outside, but instead I received the confirmation of two words: love greatly.

To love greatly seemed abstract, like a painting of colors and lines that were meant to represent a great truth. I had come to know love. I was even finding it easier to love and extend grace to those around me, but when the answer to my question of identity rested in this phrase I struggled to comprehend. I wanted to know who I was and God just kept pointing me to love, to Himself, and to walking in humility content to dwell in the land of vulnerability. The pieces of my life, He assured me, would be put to use in due time, but that the only concern in regards to my identity was simply the question, *"Would I allow myself to be a conduit of His love and grace?"*. As I agreed this was the case I was rendered "identified" and my body left the morgue and entered into a whole new world... a world of submission and love.

In some ways the puzzle was already being put together, not by my hands, but by His as I submitted to the healing of so many broken and fractured places within. As He carefully arranged and rearranged, I allowed myself to share and be shared. And the picture began to take shape almost as organically as God coming near had been. It wasn't work, it grew out of humility, out of worship, out of submission to love, and accepting the gift of Him for all that it entailed. Somewhere in all that love, my guilt and shame were drifting into the background and I was seeing more clearly the me I was under it all.

Had the teaching on finding your identity in Christ been explained how I have experienced it, the book would be short and sweet and as easy as three steps to successful Christian living. Instead, we have chosen (more times than not) to bludgeon ourselves with works and religion. The number of times I was told to just read the Bible more and pray more were countless and profited me very little. The irony is, in these last years I have learned more about God and understood more completely my identity in Him through the experience of Him; not through the Bible and study, but through His inner working on me as I submitted to His hand and through the experience of love, from Him and others.

To experience God as I have is not an emotional adventure as some might assume. It is a soul awakening. What is most incredible is that He opens my eyes and heart to something, then shows me a dream or real life example, and then it drives me to the Word to better explain what I have experienced so I can share with others. His work in me has enlightened the words of scripture and awakened a passion to know Him more. In knowing Him more, I get to see more of who He made me to be. And I think I actually might like her...

To not know who you are is an out of body experience until you realize that the very reason you feel out of sorts is because you are missing the fullness of God roaming through you. I go about my day and He meets me -- at the stoplight, in my kitchen, as the thoughts run their course in the grocery line. There is a constancy to Him that reminds me that I am His and He is actively a part of my life. I have an "other" to identify with that actually likes me, and I know that I am nothing without Him. That was what I was missing for most of my life. My true identity.

Identity growing up was about doing, striving, proving, and claiming a title. I would do whatever it took to be the best at what I laid my hands to in hopes of becoming. Becoming what? I often did not know. One thing I always dreamed of was being a writer and a singer, but those things I would keep to myself; written in that familiar code that filled my journal. They were shameful and wrong and totally unacceptable. After all, I was deathly shy. *How would I sing in public?* And writing, well, that was something people did when they retire, but it wasn't a career path. I was expected to make use of my intelligence and set a lofty goal for a profession, but I wanted to touch people and bring healing. I wanted to change lives. I knew for me books and music were a comfort when nothing else seemed to be. It was an escape, but oftentimes it was my only hope. I wanted to deliver that hope, someway, somehow.

Delivering hope and healing to people has haunted me for as long as I can remember. It has kept me from giving up on music a number of times when I am reminded of the tears of the woman listening in the coffee shop, the man who saw His lost daughter in my song and was renewed with hope of her return, the little girl who drew the picture of me singing and gave me her eleven cents as a tip. Those moments still make me smile and I have to remember that God has given me a story and that is foundational to everything I do, and that story is a testament of His love.

The puzzle of me is the story of my life. It is not a mystery if I remain honest. Every step of the process of growing up has its place in the puzzle board and every emotion felt and unfelt unfolds before me as I walk hand in hand with my Lord. Retracing the years that were stolen, the times when I numbed out the pain, recapturing the story page by page, it is the reviving of me and the writing of an epic tale describing just who it is that I am.

Some would say that I have come to a misunderstanding about my identity in Christ because I identify with my story and personhood. That to do so is purely humanistic. The truth is, there is not one part of my story that is not Him. My identity, my story, is one line after another of the lifeblood of Christ running through me. I have not always done the things I ought, but the redeeming hand of God makes the wrongs right and gives me a million reasons to celebrate His goodness and grace. The mere existence of me proves Him to be faithful and true. And my story is a journey of identification.

When I walked out of the desert I chose to take His name -- the name He emblazoned on my heart in a way that will forever change me. When I chose to follow His lead in the broken way in order to find myself in Him, I gave up all that I was for all He longed to do in me. When I came to the end of myself and realized that all my self-protection and posturing set me apart from everything I longed for, I abandoned my pride to the shockwave of humility. I now know, more than ever, I will never be the same. Turning back is not an option. I am a new creation with a whole new foundation.

There is a foundation that God lays that no man could build alone. It is sturdy and true. It defies the battering of the wickedest of weather and is the base for everything He longs to build up in us. It is love. It is Him. It is beautiful in its simplicity and fierce in its imperviousness. It is far better than anything I could build and it is imprinted with the letters YHWH.

YHWH loosely means "I AM WHO I AM." So if He Is the foundation of who I am, His name is written on the core of all I do, then my identity is Him. My story is built on the foundation of my God who is exactly who He says He is and His essence flows through all that I am. My identity is found in my story because my story is *His* story. Every foundation I tried to lay from my own works was faulty, but I now stand on Him alone. My house will stand because He is the builder of my life.

Reflecting on all that came before I can see the structure I had attempted to build; the outwardly pleasing presentation as the interior was crumbling and falling into disrepair. All the trying to be more holy and draw closer to God did not build a house upon a rock which would withstand the storms of life. His foundation was one I could not pour of my own accord. I slaved away creating, just to watch it fall. But the Master Carpenter waited for me to answer the door and allow His hammer of truth to break through the cheap layers I had erected, and carefully He chipped away at the shellac I had layered on my heart until the soft and supple muscle began to breathe once again.

CHAPTER 13

Waterfalls and Windowsills

"Deep calls to deep at the [thundering] sound of Your waterfalls; All Your breakers and Your waves have rolled over me. Yet the Lord will command His lovingkindness in the daytime, And in the night His song will be with me, A prayer to the God of my life."

-PSALM 42:7 8 AMP

One by one the sheetrock panels came down exposing the rotten 2x4s behind them. The insulation had been eaten away by rodents and other vermin, and what remained sat in piles along the bottom of the wall. It was worse than I had thought. One wall led to two, and then another and another, until all the rooms and all the walls lay open and empty; broken pipes exposed, beams on the verge of collapse, and dead things. It was obvious this was going to be a whole house gut as the water spot on the living room ceiling was nothing more than the telltale sign of more plumbing problems and more than likely, mold. From the outside, the house looked almost immaculate, but this... well, this was a disaster.

When one sets out to remodel a home, more times than not the initial impetus for change was a small thing like wanting a new shower. The shower project soon becomes a bathroom remodel and then things start to get interesting. Once a wall is opened up more problems are discovered that send you back to the hardware store, incur more time and energy, and open up the discussion to making the project slightly larger by taking care of something else while the wall is open. All these lead to larger questions of finances and time and whether or not to hire a contractor, and the conversation logically concludes with something along the lines of, "If we are going to do this, we might as well go all the way and be done with it!"

And that is how my life has been since the "awakening". I have never been one to mess around. I get things done. I have been labeled as "intense", "driven", "passionate", "determined". One thing I am not is lazy or ineffective. Most people who know me will tell you that if you want it done, and done well, have me do it. For most of my life I thrived on that need to be needed. I desired to prove my prowess in just about everything I laid my hands on, and because failure was not even an option, I excelled. I longed for the acknowledgement of my success, and I made a big deal about my accomplishments hoping (mostly in vain) to be noticed. I was loved and hated for those very reasons.

What outward success had bought me was a life with a lot of curb appeal, but one step inside and you knew something just wasn't right. It wasn't obvious at first, but before long all the linens and fabrics began to take on a moldy and musty smell. A nasty mold or fungus was growing somewhere. *But where?* So I went to the most obvious source of a water problem -- the bathroom. Sure enough, there was a leak and mold had filled the walls, floor to ceiling. What I had on my hands was not one small problem, but many problems; some small, some large enough to fill a season of an HGTV show.

When you set out on the road to healing you have some idea why you are there. You have an issue that keeps popping up, there is a crisis that needs to be overcome, there is a nagging deep down of unresolved pain, or someone flat-out tells you that you need help. There is something that starts the ball rolling. I had spent years self-analyzing myself and pretty much figured I had acknowledged all the things that had damaged me over the years. I placed my blame, said my prayers of forgiveness, and expected life to just take off like a bird set free. But my feet remained bound to the perch until fate intervened, or rather God took the liberty of revealing my chains.

I will tell you, in my pride, I was pretty sure that if something was broken or needed fixing I could and would be able to fix it. When all my hopes and dreams were yanked out from under me with little explanation I found humility by proxy. I know now that God had everything lined up, but I was as lost and confused as a girl could be. All I knew was that I had history and that story was somehow haunting the house that I had made so beautiful to the outside world. I knew the turmoil, the deadness, the anger, and all the weaknesses and shortcomings I dare not share with anyone.

Strength and resilience, when taken on as an identity, has a way of leaving you empty and cold all the while fighting the wars of everyone and everything around you. People liked to be around me because they knew I would watch out for them and protect them, assist them in whatever they needed, and that if there was a battle there would be a victory. All you had to do was tell me something was impossible or couldn't be done and I set out to prove you wrong. I was the queen of the underdogs and conqueror of the world.

My humble kingdom over time became an oligarchy where I was the sole determiner of law and order. I chose who came and went, who received assistance and when, and as queen I was untouchable and unquestioned. I was compassionate and giving so my rule appeared civil, but under it all was an unquenchable thirst for power and control, fueled by pride, insecurity and my own self-protection.

The day I encountered humility, my stomach turned at every speck of pride in me. Whoever this was that I had become needed to go, even if it cost me everything. I jumped into the waters and began swimming upstream only to be pulled from the frigid mountain stream by the hand of God as He revealed that I would not be able to swim in the shallowness of the creek. I felt silly and humiliated. So, I laced up my hiking shoes, humbled myself and began to follow; one step at a time, in the footsteps of my Lord.

I had pretty much predetermined, due to my extensive hours on the self-help aisle at the bookstore, that my problems were due to two sexual encounters and possibly some issues with how my mother and I related. But like any good adventure in repair, one thing led to another and every day became a new undertaking of pain, sorrow, grief, and healing of wounds. It was terrifying and glorious all at once. In a matter of days whole sections of my life would be torn down, assessed, and the repairs would begin.

When your life, your house, has been unkempt for long periods of time you forget all the little things you overlooked over the years -- the screw that fell out of the cabinet where the door now hangs askew, the drip of the faucet that would have just needed a new washer years ago, but now needs to be completely replaced. The satire in my sordid tale was that I had neglected myself in much the same ways I had felt neglected by others over the years.

As the walls came down, and love filled the air, for the first time I didn't feel neglected or alone or even ashamed. As the healing commenced and all I had was humility to walk forward in, I was broken. Broken, but in awe. And as heart wrenching as the demolition and redesign was, it awakened the passions and desires I had stuffed away so many years ago. And the tears... well, they came easier and easier as my heart became more supple and warm.

The picture that fills my mind when I think about how healing has felt is another one of those moving pictures:

I see a window with a bench below it. I take a seat and longingly look out the window at the most amazing view. As I allow my mind to wander, dreams begin to take form and I can see them unfold just beyond the glass. It is like they are there for my observation only, and deep within I fear that I will never take hold of them. And then the tears begin to fall in the knowing that to acquire the dream I must leave the house. Sure the house is cold and dark, but I am used to it -- it makes me tougher. A light rain begins to fall and like the tears of God they roll down the window, as my pain pools on the inside of the windowsill. There is a distance between us that my facade and walls of protection have created. To open the window would mean to let the rain in, allow the winds of change to blow through, and I would be tempted to crawl out and take hold of the dream. It would mean exposure. *What if everything changed?* Looking around I acknowledge that the only risk would be losing something I didn't really value a whole lot anyway. The rain stops and the clouds break. I struggle within, weigh the risk of possibility, and slowly raise my hand and place it on the windowsill. A long deep breath is followed by sliding the window up just enough so that the fresh air could slip under. It is intoxicating and I have to have more. The freshness draws my head and then my body out the window and my dirty bare feet land safely on the lush green grass below. And almost without warning I am scooped up, spun around, and all I can hear is the laughter of my loving Father as He tells me how He has longed for me to come close. And then He walks me out into the beauty.

And that is how it felt climbing out of darkness. I had all of these fears that held no merit. A lifetime of keeping myself in prison not understanding that vulnerability would not destroy me rather it would revive me. It left me in complete wonder as each step of the healing process seemed natural and full of peace. To be seen and known was my biggest fear, but what I found was that to be exposed was not so that I would be rejected, but so I could be accepted in full. I had lived as half a person; emotionally turned off, physically striving for approval, internally fractured, and spiritually distant. Everything, absolutely everything, was different and changing. Where once a smile was something I put on, it now radiated on its own accord. Where defenses rose for all to see, a soft more attractive person stood. I was changing and the world was taking notice.

When things begin changing on the inside you often wonder if anyone else can tell. You know your view of things has changed, that you have better clarity, feel more stable and more joyful, but the question remains. *Does anyone else notice?* As my transformation began to take place that question was answered immediately. Sunday after Sunday I would go to church and be greeted by people who wanted to know what was going on with me because I was radiating this joy. I had no idea what that looked like, but I trusted the inward changes were piercing through my once substantial armor. One by one the conversations happened, and before long I had about twenty people who were regularly checking in with me.

What I had not understood was God's plan. When I stepped back into church (after a very long hiatus), I knew I needed community. It was really the only reason that I had for pushing hard against the pressure to remain on my island of isolation. One step of obedience was met with the guiding hand of God. I gave Him my heart and He not only guarded and protected it, but nurtured and cared for it. As I was reintroduced to leading worship, He put me in front of a church full of people who were instantly drawn to my talents, but equally intrigued by the mystery of me. They watched as my heart became more and more exposed; more angst *and* freedom of expression overall. There was even a sensual quality that came through that I was completely unaware (or I would have been mortified). As I was removed from leading, the congregation was completely incognizant. A month went by and I began to play again on teams, but not leading and people began asking me when I would lead again. It was flattering, but completely devastating all at once. This was when the real healing began.

Every Sunday people would come and tell me how my voice and demeanor and presence had changed. Then the next week they would comment again, almost as if they were in as much shock and surprise as I was. All I could do was smile and laugh, and hug, and smile some more. And then I knew... this journey was for me, but was also for so many more. I have learned that God doesn't go about healing us so that we can just feel better, but so that there is a testament of Him for the world to see.

Near the summit of the mountain of God are many glaciers, and those sheets of thick ice melt under the warming glow of the sun. The crisp cool waters carve out a path down the mountain in babbling brooks and cascading waterfalls. You always know when you are getting close to a waterfall on your trek, you can hear it. It's like a siren singing through the forest beckoning you to discover its origins. There is always the temptation to veer off the trail to sneak a peek, but the thundering from beyond reminds you of the payoff for all your hard work if you stay the course, so you keep walking.

I am a nature girl through and through. And water, well, you can try to keep me away from it, but it always calls to me. I have spent a lot of time hiking in some of the most amazing places. I am always in awe of what I find, because though I set out with a map and a pretty good idea of what I will discover, there is always something that takes my breath away or I stumble upon that "once in a lifetime" experience. Now that I have taken on the title of amateur photographer I capture some of those moments and bring them back to share, but so many moments you cannot capture but in your mind and memory. This journey has been much the same. Even the pages of my journal don't contain half of what I have taken in, processed, or walked through, but the changed life, no one can deny.

Something amazing and wonderful has happened along this journey of vulnerability and healing. I have found peace and friends I would have never imagined knowing. More importantly, I found family in God Himself, and a wholeness in my surrender to His authority in my life. I feel like a broken record, but I found life in His love.

The story would be perfect to end there, but then it would be incomplete. I would rob you of the most stunning part of the tale. The part where princess meets her prince.

CHAPTER 14

My Beloved

""Listen! My beloved! Behold, he comes, Climbing on the mountains, Leaping and running on the hills! "My beloved is like a gazelle or a young stag. Behold, he is standing behind our wall, He is looking through the windows, He is gazing through the lattice. "My beloved speaks and says to me, 'Arise, my love, my fair one, And come away. 'For behold, the winter is past, The rain is over and gone. 'The flowers appear on the earth once again; The time for singing has come, And the voice of the turtledove is heard in our land. 'The fig tree has budded and ripens her figs, And the vines are in blossom and give forth their fragrance. Arise, my love, my fair one, And come away [to climb the rocky steps of the hillside].'"

~SONG OF SOLOMON 2:8-13 AMP

I was not a girly girl by any measure as a child, but like every little girl I had dreams that I would someday be whisked away by my prince and I would live happily ever after. After years and years of disappointment I was pretty sure I was a very disillusioned little girl; brainwashed by the likes of Disney, Hallmark, and Anne of Green Gables. I bring new meaning to the phrase "hopeless romantic". The truth was, I did everything in my power to run from my prince. I was self-sufficient, self-protective, self-reliant, self-contained… I had eliminated every need that a prince would need to fill.

So when I found myself alone and vulnerable and fully admitting to my weaknesses and shortcomings, I feared that I would be taken advantage of like I had been in the past. The one true intimate encounter that I had been vulnerable enough to engage in overran me and destroyed me all at once, when "no" had no longer meant "no" I was rendered powerless and broken. It haunted me every time I allowed anyone close. I would raise my defenses, lock my castle up tight, and silently weep dry tears for all that I would never have.

As my heart began to soften and melt and God came close, I feared the intimacy. *What if this new view of God was just as faulty as my old one? What if I was just making God into my spiritual "boyfriend" so I could feel better about myself? What if everything I was thinking and feeling was really all just heresy and I was signing my own death certificate by believing it? What if God was who He said He was -- a jealous lover of my soul, constant and loyal companion, passionately in pursuit of me, and longing for the best for me in every area of my life?* The questions all fought for my attention, but the final one drew me...

As a child, Song of Solomon was off limits and of course my little mind wanted to know why. So I opened the pages of my Bible and read. There were words that seemed dirty and wrong. It was poetic, but it didn't make much sense. It was pretty much the same experience I had when we had been warned that we were not to watch the movie "Dirty Dancing". I saw people dancing and couldn't figure out what made it "dirty", but I had been told it was. I was naive (to a fault) and couldn't grasp the larger picture of either forbidden fruit. Why we choose to shelter instead of educating our children properly, I may never know, but for me it meant it was up to me to discover truth and guidance.

Truth and guidance come from knowledge and maturity, in the absence of those things you get a random education that will have holes the size of Texas throughout, and it isn't until you reach midlife that you finally see the deficiencies. And that was me. Having crossed into the forties and realizing that the foundation wasn't cracked, a great deal of it was never laid or missing altogether.

As God began to re-lay the foundation and make the necessary repairs to my wounded heart, the feelings that I had stuffed down so deep began to bubble up to the surface like springs pressing through the layers of terra firma aspiring to reach their end outside of the earth's crust. The feelings were welcome, but had no place to rest.

Emotions lead one to intimacy, but when the foundations of intimacy are broken, shattered, or missing you have a hard time managing the new friends who have come to visit. There is no bed for them to lie, and try as you may to contain them, they demand an environment where they can grow and thrive, not just a place to be shelved and admired. They surface and make themselves known so that we will share them and grow together with one another through them. It is not housing them, rather it is facilitating their maintenance and discovering their beauty.

The foundation stone of healthy intimacy when no model has ever stood before you will be non-existent. And if you are like me, your reference points for closeness and intimacy have been tainted with danger, distrust, and abuse. To understand intimacy a whole new foundation would have to be established. I was eager to understand, but scared at what that might require of me.

The requirements of intimacy were not as scary as I had dreamed up in my mind. There would be a relearning of healthy physical intimacy, but emotionally… God had already begun to pour the foundation of that one. It was truth, vulnerability, and the complete giving of oneself.

Truth and vulnerability have become a staple of my life, and in some ways I feel like to live now any other way would be a form of treason. The higher my commitment to truth and honesty the more free I become. No sane person would trade life and freedom for the chains of deceit and hiding, especially once they taste what freedom is like. It is sweet. It is savory. It teases the taste buds and leaves us longing for more. And that is why I believe with all my heart that if you truly knew God you would not be able to walk away. Even on the worst day, you would desire Him.

I had been reading (as I probably do too often) and God reached out and tapped me on the shoulder. Not physically, but I knew He was near and asking me for a moment of His attention. I put down my book and sat quietly. A smile drew itself across my face and my heart grew warm and full. I chuckled to myself. He had come for me… just for me.

There is something about knowing that you are being pursued in a loving way, that just brings a smile to your face at the silliest of times. The desire of the suitor awakens even the deadest of souls. When into the room comes a spark of hope that I may actually be desirable and possibly even loveable, the heart can't help but skip a beat. And that was how I found myself; a little dumbfounded that I was worthy of the attention, but blushing at the thought of knowing this beau. He was relentless in His pursuit and I could not ignore His advances.

When the Lord catches your attention, pulls your eye in His direction, and you see the passion in His eyes there is something so tantalizing that to ignore it would be to silence every longing and desire within. I realize that some people will want to burn me at the stake for what I am about to say, but I cannot deny my own life experience. It is part of my story, His story, our story.

The day I realized that I had not been wandering out in the desert alone stirred in me fear. *Why had this man been watching me, following me, but never helping me? And where along my journey did he take notice and choose to follow my winding path through the sand?* Visions of terror danced a wild ritual around the fire of my soul, as I kept one eye on the horizon and one on this strange, but intriguing man who hung back just far enough that to see his face was impossible, but one could tell his form was strong.

History had spoken to my heart to not slow down, to not allow the stranger to approach or come any closer. As the scorching sun beat down and scalded my exposed limbs, my mouth grew dry, and I soon was moving at no more than a crawl. I looked out to see the man, still walking confidently, still keeping a distance so as to not frighten or intimidate me. On my hands and knees I felt foolish, and a bitterness began to rise up from the belly of me. *If this man was strong and respectful, why was he not rescuing me in my time of need?* There was a coldness that bit like a snake at the surface of my heart. *This man, like all the others, would stand by and watch me fail and laugh at my folly.* I turned my eyes to the horizon and determined that I would reach the promise if it was the last thing I did.

Day after day, night after night, I dug down into the depths of human strength and pathetically crawled across the arid and parched land. Every time I looked back, there he stood. I was becoming quite frustrated by his inactivity and I began to shout across the desert, "If you are so strong, why don't you carry me to my destination?" And to my question there would be no reply, just the steady steps that matched mine.

Days turned to months and months into years. The desert seemed endless and foreboding. My skin had been wrecked by the constant exposure, my body weary from endless miles of suffering, and my heart and mind were seared by the years of stubborn determination under the intense heat of the sun. As I felt my body on the verge of collapse I turned one last time and looked over my shoulder, half expecting the man to have fled. But there he stood.

I cried out one last time, this time as a plea and not to taunt, "If you have any compassion at all, please help me." And to my surprise he slowly began to move closer to where I had come to rest. My heart began to race. To accept defeat and ask for help was counter to every decision that had been made prior. As he approached I watched, uncertain if I would accept his help even if he readily gave it.

He was tall, dark skinned, a rugged man. There was a calmness to his demeanor and a steadiness to his step, and an overwhelming sense of nobility that hung on him like a fine garment. The closer he came, the more at ease I felt, which was odd seeing as how closeness had always been threatening to me.

When he was a few yards from me, he stopped. I feared it was because he realized his error and that I was not the person he thought he had been following all along. But as I looked up, his eyes pierced the heart of me. His face did not hold confusion or even a look of inconvenience. In his eyes was a love that reflected like a glassy sea, as a tear crested the lid and slowly ran its course over the surface of his cheek, losing itself in the growth of a beard in need of a good trim. "Please help me." My plea rang out from the most desperate part of my soul.

He quietly took in the scene, and more tears came to his eyes. I was confused. *Why was he not scooping me up and carrying me out of the desert?* He knelt down and our eyes met on level. Everything in me surged with knowing as I realized that tears were coming to my eyes as well. And as we exchanged a long minute eye to eye, I knew he knew the deepest parts of me. How? I did not know, but I knew he was not mistaken by my appearance. I was who he had come for.

"You know I am not well. I am tired and broken. I just need to get out of the sun. To find a shelter from this place." As much as I wanted his tenderness to reach out and take hold of me, I threw up my defenses. He kept his distance, but watched me with the deepest compassion in his features, like he was waiting for something. "What is it you want from me?" My anger lashed out like a whip, but still he knelt looking into my eyes as if he was trying to draw water from a well. *Why was he so reticent?*

I studied him once again. "If you see my pain, my plight in this barren land, why don't you rescue me?" Again he stayed silent, but the tears began to fall like a cascade of a mighty waterfall from his sensitive gaze. I reached out my hand in a desperate effort. I really have no idea why I extended my arm, maybe it was the exhaustion from years of wandering, but maybe it was the desire deep down to be seen, to be known. And as if I had unlocked his vocal cords he spoke, " Oh, my dear friend! You're so beautiful! And your eyes so beautiful. Get up, my dear friend..."

His words were foreign, like spices unfamiliar to my palate. I took them in, tasted their strange flavor, and as I did he ever so gently took hold of my outstretched hand. As my skin touched his I felt a wave of warmth flow through me. It was unlike anything I had experienced before. It was comforting. It was enveloping, and my mind began to race as my heart kept time. *What was this curious feeling threatening to overtake my sanity?* My heart leapt.

"Get up, my dear friend." His words echoed once again and my bones and muscles were compelled to follow his instruction. Again he spoke, "Get up, my dear friend, my fair and beautiful lover -- come to me!" I was embarrassed, confused, and blushing in delight all at once. As I arose he spoke yet again, "Come, my shy and modest dove -- leave your seclusion, come... let me see your face, let me hear your voice. For your voice is soothing and your face ravishing." His words made me squirm in the uncertainty of his proposition. It was as if he already knew me, but I had not known him. *Was this man completely insane?* I had to find out, for the love he exuded was more than I could take.

His eyes held fast to mine as he continued, "You're beautiful from head to toe, my dear love, beautiful beyond compare, absolutely flawless. Come with me... my bride." His words rang with the deepest of desire, but I could not understand them. I was not a worthy bride, my failings numbered the sands of the desert and my countenance was anything but beautiful, and moreover I was defiled. I was sure by this time that this man was, in fact, ripely out of his mind. "Abandon your wilderness seclusion, where you keep company with lions and panthers guard your safety. You've captured my heart, dear friend. You looked at me, and I fell in love. One look my way and I was hopelessly in love! How beautiful your love, dear, dear friend..."

What had I done to warrant this attention? I longed for relief from the desert, to be taken to safety, and allowed one more day to live. I was not seeking a bridegroom. I had no intention of drawing close or revealing myself to anyone, let alone this strange man pursuing me through the desert and wilderness. But he was relentless in his pursuit of me. And as he took my hand and looked deeply into my eyes piercing my heart, the throbbing just beyond my ribcage pulsed a new song. A song with no words, strange and unfamiliar, yet alive and very much from my heart of hearts.

Our first encounters were respectfully loving in every way. I would smile and he would nod and smile back at me. He would wait for me to agree to move and then escorted me. He wrapped his arm around my quaking shoulder as the night tried to steal my peace. He pulled me near and spoke words so sweet and tender reassuring me that I was safe and secure in his arms. There was soon no place I would rather be, but with my beloved and he with me.

Without a word he knew my heart, yet he longed to hear me share the deeper things I held within and never once did his attention waver. It was as if I was the only one in his world, the apple of his eye, the desire of his heart. He had chosen me in the desert of my wandering, then cherished me like a stunning jewel, protected me like a mighty warrior, nurtured me as a tender rose, provided for my every need, always placing his emphasis on what would be best for *me*. And most of all, his love was pure and true.

I had never felt so valuable, so humbled that such a one of obvious royalty would find me attractive and worthy, yet even in the presence of such a tangible love I doubted it would remain. And time and time again he would reassure me of his love and his intention to spend eternity with me. His steadfastness amazed me, and his patience in my hours of doubt were like a fine drink of water. He never did once leave me.

It was peculiar, this man's unending love even in the face of opposition and my disbelief. *How could he continue to love one such as me? How could he lavish on me the magnificence of all he was, seeking nothing in return?* And day by day, I found myself longing; desiring to believe, to draw closer to him and to know his heart. I had an insatiable need to understand this stranger whose passion was only for me.

He wooed me in the depths of my despair, pulled me close and comforted my weary heart and mended my fractured trust. Then one day as he sang over me. The ice that had encapsulated my heart began to melt, and a puddle of tears filled his hands. He captured my heart and held my wounds, and the hardness that disallowed my passion to rise was no more. I jumped into his arms with abandon, longing to feel his warmth and to know his touch, to hear his heart and know its pulse as the rhythm of life itself. There was nothing that could draw my sight from him, not the most stunning of sunsets or the sparkle of a priceless diamond. My heart was alive! Love broke forth with a devotion unrivaled by any I had felt before and the anticipation… I needed to experience the ecstasy of a life remaining in him. I believed him for all he was and I pledged myself to him saying, "I am my lover's. I'm all he wants. I'm all the world to him! Come, dear lover— let's tramp through the countryside. Let's sleep at some wayside inn, then rise early and listen to bird-song. Let's look for wildflowers in bloom, blackberry bushes blossoming white, Fruit trees festooned with cascading flowers. And there I'll give myself to you, my love to your love!"

The embrace of love stripped the covering of sin and shame leaving me wonderfully vulnerable in the security of my bridegroom. I was my beloved's and he was mine. It blew all limits of understanding, and in his arms of love I instinctively knew that he would never leave me or forsake me. I knew that this intimacy was true, that his touch upon my life was deep and pure and I was his bride -- now and forevermore, to love and cherish. And I knew I would be honored to do the same for him.

Unlike so many fairy tales where princes take princesses, this story does not end at the wedding, not even at the marriage supper, but continues on for all eternity -- each giving and being given one to another, in a seamless union of love, knit together in truth, and wrapped in an intimacy of trust. It is far greater than my imagination could have conjured up, and far more complete than any love my heart could have known.

He had followed me from my infancy, chose me before I could have ever known of Him, and dedicated His pursuit to bringing to me the fullness of life. His loving kindness, His passionate pursuit, His care and overt concern for my well-being, conquered my every fear and satisfied every desire of my heart. I will never ever be the same.

There is a smile I feel on the surface of my heart, that I know is not something I knew before. A longing to share every vestige of my life with the Lover of my soul, to reveal every piece of me in complete surrender to all that He is, to know Him in His fullness as I surrender myself to His will. I had no idea of my need until I was shown what I lacked, and showered in the astounding abundance of His love. I would be a lonely princess no more now that my Prince had come.

CHAPTER 15

The Pronouncement of Beauty

"The Spirit of the Lord God is upon me, Because the Lord has anointed and commissioned me To bring good news to the humble and afflicted; He has sent me to bind up [the wounds of] the brokenhearted, To proclaim release [from confinement and condemnation] to the [physical and spiritual] captives And freedom to prisoners, To proclaim the favorable year of the Lord , And the day of vengeance and retribution of our God, To comfort all who mourn, To grant to those who mourn in Zion the following: To give them a turban instead of dust [on their heads, a sign of mourning], The oil of joy instead of mourning, The garment [expressive] of praise instead of a disheartened spirit. So they will be called the trees of righteousness [strong and magnificent, distinguished for integrity, justice, and right standing with God], The planting of the Lord, that He may be glorified."

~ISAIAH 61:1-3 AMP

Beauty, when you have believed you are unbeautiful, or when you have sought to make yourself unattractive, either consciously or subconsciously, holds connotations that stir up the dust of past neglect and/or abuse. When I was confronted with the word beautiful it meant sex appeal. A word used to manipulate me and enslave me. It had nothing to do with the dictionary definition, though I was well familiar, it had been redefined through my experiences.

When God begins to speak your beauty over you it makes your heart flutter. Really, it does. I don't care how messed up in the head you are, there is not a girl on this planet who can resist the truthfulness of a perfect God calling her beautiful. We can hardly tune out human affirmation, let alone God's.

It is really like a butterfly emerging from the unassuming cocoon and unfurling its wings to dry them in the breeze under the warmth of the sun. Even at just its reveal we are awestruck by the colors that were not manifest when they were wrapped tightly in the cocoon.

We begin by inching along like the poor caterpillar, the statistics not great for our survival in a world full of predators and poison, and through great trial and temptation we reach our end (or at least we think). When the caterpillar begins to spin his cocoon do you really think he believes that he is dying? How could he not? Using all his energy stores, he builds his own coffin and climbs inside. It is death, death leading to a new glorious life of flight that a crawling thing could not even imagine. It is by faith that he follows the order of things.

We may not know what lies ahead, but if the past is any indication, it only gets better, free-er, and more magnificent as we walk in obedience to the One who knows this life beginning to end. We will climb mountains, traverse valleys, swim mighty oceans that threaten to drown us in our sorrows, but He will never leave us. His hand will guide us into all truth. He will reconstruct the decrepit structures we have become. Through every high and low He is faithful. He is love, and love, well, it never fails.

The day that it dawned; when the sun crested the mountain and the sky shone with a ripple of quilted red, demanding I stop and take in the fullness of what was; there was an awe that caught me up. It was wonder, the part of me that had been dormant all these years. It was like God opened the heavens and said, "This," His arms opening wide in presentation, "This is my gift to you."

And I smiled.

And He laughed with pleasure.

And I cried.

And He smiled.

And then I smiled and laughed.

"I love you."

"I know." I replied.

"I have always loved you... with an everlasting love." His gaze unmistakable, my heart quaking in the reality. "I have been waiting to give you the greater gifts. I have not been withholding my love as you have supposed. What I am giving you today required all of you to receive. You are ready now."

And then I knew... life would never be the same. I had not reached the peak just yet, but I didn't care. I was holding what I had come for -- love. When I had set out on the journey, I longed for a sense of peace, but I had no idea what it was I *actually* needed. Taking in all of who He was in that moment -- overwhelming.

In life there is resurrection. It is the moment when the soul, once hard and unyielding, comes to a place of humility; where pliability is the only desire, and to be known is the motivation for everything. The intrinsic thought that this new vulnerable reality, as counter as it is to what all history had laid down before, is what my heart has sought all along. Truth.

As I had spent years hiding, my God had been pursuing. As I grabbed my sword and lunged at the air, fighting to show that I didn't care, God knew the ache I denied within. He knew the hurt I had shut out and how I had shutdown. He knew the story. He knew *my* story. And even when I thought He was far off, He had been there. He had cried the tears that I would not and could not feel. He whispered comfort in the night that I was too deaf in my own disappointments to hear. The Lover of my soul had been chasing me down, desiring my whole heart, and here we were staring into the brilliance of a new day... Together. Complete. One.

To say that vulnerability, the complete exposure of being known, takes courage... well, in hindsight I would have to agree. As I walked each day, shedding yet another layer under which I had sought to hide away, my steps were conscious and cautious. My awe of the many small miracles drew me further and further into truth. I would literally wake up and say, "If it is this good now, I can't wait until tomorrow." And another piece of my protective gear would be left somewhere along the mountain trail.

When this all began, I told God (jokingly of course) that if this journey ended up being about vulnerability, "I'm out." Yet the moment I had said it, I knew. As I wrote day after day the truth He so desperately wanted to show me -- that the imperative to love (what I desired more than anything) was found in vulnerability -- I knew the day would come. And I told Him, "If you make me write a book about vulnerability..." followed by a knowing laugh, "Well, it will be the most epic story of my life." And epic story it has become.

When you set out on a journey, you rarely know where the path will take you. It starts with heartache and defeat, that place where you are confident that the end is near, not the beginning. It feels a lot more like breaking than fixing. The heart feels raw and battered and its pulse has become irregular. There is little hope, but you hold onto the one tiny glimmer of light on the horizon. And as you fix your gaze, every wound begins to shout. You know that death is but a breath away, but you extend that arm, take hold of a handful of sand and claw your way forward across the barren desert. The desperation to know that elusive light draws and compels as everything in you screams for the madness to stop and to accept things as they are; to just give up.

It was the light, the piercing goodness and grace and love that called out into my night. It was the purity that sought to scour out the grime that walking through a wasteland had gathered within my soul and upon my flesh. It was everything I feared knowing God would be and more.

When you come to the place of complete surrender, when all life's contents have been thrown out on the table and nothing is left hidden, there is a satisfaction and a peace that had you told me I would not have believed you. To be known, well, there is nothing like it in the whole world. To try to place words on it is nearly impossible. It is like freedom, but it is covenant. It is being overwhelmed by love all the while compelled to give it all away. It makes no sense, yet it makes all the sense in the world. It is living.

Living takes dying. Dying to myself, my self-defenses, my need to rule and reign, my self-confidence, and my history. My dying was what He had been waiting for all along. I had foolishly believed He wanted my sacrifice of service and the false humility of my martyrdom, but like a good suitor He was waiting for truth. My truth. He knew that the relationship could not be manifested in its fullness without the complete revealing of my nakedness before I could fully accept the nature of Him and His truth.

In His pursuit of me He showed me more and more of Himself, the more I allowed myself to be seen. It was a beautiful courtship dance that continuously lured me. The innocence of curiosity, the desire to know Him more, the chasing after the moments of newfound love and desire, the beauty preparations of the soul to make ready the bride for the bridegroom... it all came so fast. I had not even been looking for a groom, I had eyes for another, for the world, but He desired me. Not for who I was in that moment, covered in layers of deceit and striving, but for who He knew I was deep down. He saw to the heart of me --a heart He wanted all for His own, for His selfish pleasure, but also to share our union with the world. I was what He had come to receive. His beautiful bride. I had no idea that was me until it was. Now I can't wait to see what this life together will bring.

It is going to be truly epic!

Afterword

When I set out to climb the mountain of God I sought a new revelation. I wanted, no, needed to know, was He real. Faith alone spoke to my mind and I believed that if I were to embark upon the journey that some spiritual illumination would come to my soul. I was seeking peace and love and maybe a better life, if that was possible. My thoughts, my motivations were selfish and for the pacifying of my own carnal condition. I had no idea that what I sought was salvation. I thought I had that. And though, at times, it was unfulfilling and left me wanting, I had determined it had been my own inability to meet the requirements to attain the desired result. In a way, I was correct. My life; spiritually, mentally, and physically had only been lived in parts because of fear.

Fear, when I look back, is all I knew. I feared rejection, abandonment, aloneness, my humanness, failure, to be seen as weak, dependence, independence. I feared not knowing enough, knowing too much, hurting others and being hurt by them. I feared community, to be known... vulnerability, but most of all I feared love. Which is the greatest irony of all given that was all I desired from the beginning -- to know, truly know love.

I am happy to say, I now know love. I realize my beauty. I am betrothed to the most amazing groom a bride could ever hope for. Everyday He takes my hand, looks me in the eyes, stares deep into my soul, and guides me deeper into the depths of His love. It requires my compliance to the mandate of vulnerability, but that hardly seems like effort when you know He always has your best in mind.

I used to hold onto the quote, "Love is seeking the highest good in another". The cynic in me believed it was a good thought, longed to see it, but believed it was meant to simply motivate us to try harder at self sacrifice. I laugh because that is simply not true. When we read what love is in 1 Corinthians 13 it is not a list of "to dos" it is the character of God. For He... He *is* love.

It is my hope that as you have read this story that something has touched you, stirred you to deeper longing, unearthed places in your soul you have buried deep and hidden away. If all these words have been just letters on a page, I have sorely missed the mark and I am sorry to have wasted your precious time. My prayer is that my life written in these pages is a testament to my God, if it is anything else, may He deal with me justly. It is by His love I have followed through with this step of obedience. May you be blessed.

"Even though I walk through the [sunless] valley of the shadow of death, I fear no evil, for You are with me; Your rod [to protect] and Your staff [to guide], they comfort and console me. You prepare a table before me in the presence of my enemies. You have anointed and refreshed my head with oil; My cup overflows. Surely goodness and mercy and unfailing love shall follow me all the days of my life, And I shall dwell forever [throughout all my days] in the house and in the presence of the Lord."

~PSALM 23:4-6 AMP

www.ingramcontent.com/pod-product-compliance
Lightning Source LLC
LaVergne TN
LVHW061223100826
845148LV00004B/843

* 9 7 9 8 9 8 5 3 0 2 9 0 5 *